T0032385

BEST CANADIAN POETRY 2024

BARDIA SINAEE, GUEST EDITOR

ANITA LAHEY, SERIES EDITOR

BIBLIOASIS

WINDSOR, ONTARIO

FIRST EDITION
ISBN 978-1-77196-568-2 (Trade Paper)
ISBN 978-1-77196-569-9 (eBook)

Guest edited by Bardia Sinaee
Series edited by Anita Lahey
Editors-at-large: Michael Fraser, Laboni Islam
Editorial assistant: Ashley Van Elswyk
Copyedited by Sohini Ghose
Series designed by Ingrid Paulson
Typeset by Vanessa Stauffer

Published with the generous assistance of the Canada Council for the Arts, which last year invested $153 million to bring the arts to Canadians throughout the country, and the financial support of the Government of Canada. Biblioasis also acknowledges the support of the Ontario Arts Council (OAC), an agency of the Government of Ontario, which last year funded 1,709 individual artists and 1,078 organizations in 204 communities across Ontario, for a total of $52.1 million, and the contribution of the Government of Ontario through the Ontario Book Publishing Tax Credit and Ontario Creates.

PRINTED AND BOUND IN CANADA

CONTENTS

Anita Lahey

FOREWORD

Ways and Means of Escape

One weekend last year, my brother invited my son and me to join him and his daughters on an escape-room escapade. I was dubious. I imagined being shut into a locked, unwelcoming space, where I would be confronted with puzzles to solve before someone let me out. Why would I pay to do this?

And yet, their enthusiasm awoke my curiosity. Matt and the girls live in Burlington, Ontario, where they'd already "solved" so many of the local options that we had to branch out. We settled on an outfit Milton. Our options for kid-appropriate scenarios included a superhero crisis, a tomb raiders expedition, and a foray into the wizarding world. (The variety in themes was my first clue there was more to this than I'd guessed.) The cousins—all three at prime Harry Potter–fan age—went for magic. We drove from one suburb to another and parked at a strip mall, my preconceived notions of being trapped in dismal surroundings rearing as we pulled in.

Forty minutes later, the five of us each stood poised by buttons on the wall that, when pressed, emitted animal sounds. "Wait, quiet," Matt was saying, tense, alert. "OK, on three. Again!" And he activated the pattern we'd deduced we had to replicate, then pointed to us one by one. The noises rang out: *meeow, croak, hoot-hoot*! Nothing. Wrong again.

"That's not it," my niece, then ten, insisted. "I know what to do!"

We were in an elaborate stage set: a magic shop. We stood among wands, broomsticks, a massive spell book, a bookshelf crammed with jars bearing labels such as "bat's wings" and "eye of newt," an illustrated map of an imaginary land, and a grid of witch portraits. We'd gained entry from the cobbled street outside through solving several puzzles embedded in a wizard-world "reality." There were keys to reveal, drawers to unlock, padlocks to decode. Once inside, we'd deduced a pattern among potions and deciphered runes into spells. Now we stood anxiously by these animal-sound buttons. Time was running out. Matt traded places with his daughter.

My niece activated the sequence. We followed her lead. A box popped open. She'd cracked it!

A little while later, we emerged from the wizard world giddy, dazed, a bit wrecked, like people unbuckling at the end of a rollercoaster ride.

*

Welcome to the sixteenth annual edition of *Best Canadian Poetry*, an "escape" experience of a different kind altogether.

The poems in this anthology are arranged alphabetically by title. You may, if you choose, read the poems in order, as they land. In that case you'd begin, this year, with the first lines of Sarah Yi-Mei Tsiang's "The air, then":

I am 100 years pregnant, old as a tree

that must pry up its roots
to wade through the swamp-air.

Just three lines in, and you're transformed: a tree in a swamp, a century old, preparing to wrench itself free. You're a woman feeling the full weight and consequence of the life forming within her, and the gravity of what lies ahead.

The promise of birth in Tsiang's poem is followed by Carolyn Smart's "Ashes," in which grief is handed over (along with the corresponding ashes) in what could be "a shopping bag, with handles."

The next piece is "Atmospheric River," Nicholas Bradley's missive from within the thick of a profoundly unsettling climate-change-related weather event.

As such, in the first three poems of this book, through no curatorial intervention, we find ourselves embedded first in life's beginning, then in its end, and finally, smack in the midst of the terror in between.

But there is no theme or chronology to compel this way of engaging with the anthology. You could fan the pages—the escape room was like this, a cascade of possibilities before us, where to start?—and let the book fall open at "A Cartographer Maps His Way Out of His Country," by Olajide Salawu, where you'll follow a harrowing route that includes a very different river—"a huge jar of tears"—and a government that "advises there is no need for us to / think of water."

You might land on "5 A.M.," Michael Ondaatje's poem dedicated to Stan Dragland and Kris Coleman, in which you'll spin into "The wilderness of our youth, an empty barn / dancing with friends into the small hours …"

Flip to the Ls. In "Last Train Home," James Scoles writes, "I'm buzzing with the energy of a / dying fluorescent tube as two lovers / duck out of our car…" Does your buzzing self stay in the car, or follow the lovers out the door?

"Moving Day," by Susan Gillis, ushers in a blast of frustration that moves in like a sudden storm front: "Hilltop, apple tree, broken / bench, damn you, weather, damn you."

Meghan Kemp-Gee's "A Newly Discovered Species of Lizard with Distinctive Triangular Scales," begins, "I am Charles Darwin. I eat owlflesh at Cambridge University." Stop. Read the line again. Charles Darwin. Owlflesh. In the first person. *I*. There is no aloofness here. No holding to yourself, as you were before. This is another kind of evolution, internal, occurring at the pace of your reading eye.

Skipping ahead, to poems that begin with "S," Erin Conway-Smith starts us off in "Still, Night Thoughts," her poem of intense but quiet reckoning—"hush" is a word she employs—with "A fresh metre between fact and feeling": a cold, wet blanket of snow that I, as a reader, want to burrow into, looking for, well, I don't yet know. Pine grosbeaks in greyscale. A truck stop. A wolf. Something about how "Winter disappears the house…"

The snowflakes in Jean Eng's "Tai Chi in the Snow" are not the kind that pile up. They're "stars" that dissolve on a shoulder. I see them, one after another, melting into splotches before they disappear. From one element, to another, to another. The person in the poem is an object lodged between sky and earth, interrupting the snowflakes' fall, seeing not snowflakes but stars. Or, rather, both. Holding both to be true at once. And making, by the pure heat rising from within the body, both truths dissolve.

Any poem in this anthology could provoke its own journey—its own experiential immersion—akin to the one prompted by Eng's snowflakes, Yi-Mei Tsiang's profoundly pregnant narrator, or any of the other examples I've shared. What makes these poems "best"? That is a question for this year's intrepid, astute, determined guest editor, Bardia Sinaee, and you'll find a refreshingly bold answer to it in his Introduction. You'll also find his deeply considered, thought-provoking, and poignant answer to artificial intelligence (AI) and its relationship to poetry and poets going forward. Using some powerful examples from the poems collected here, Sinaee discusses how poetry makes things "real," which might sound contradictory to the tenuous connection I'm making here between poetry and the imaginary world of an escape room. It's not. His own book *Intruder*, which won the Trillium Book Award for Poetry in 2022, provides convenient proof. The poems within are an engrossing blend of bare commentary and myth; of plain-spoken observation with conjecture, reaction, lament, bemusement, philosophical enquiry (at times hilarious in its self-deprecation), openness, warmth, and play. These multiplicities, paradoxically, sharpen our perception as we read and, by extension, sharpen reality. In this brief excerpt below from "Ample Habitat," Sinaee walks us through a vivid environment punctuated with a poignant, fanciful metaphor. It's a dose of reality butting up against a deftly harnessed imagination, the effect of which requires no explanation, and simultaneously defies it:

> ...Hating on this city
> is a rite of passage I embrace
> to demonstrate my love. City of delays,

egregious detours, great rebar
obstacle courses; of mid-rises aging
without grace, like tulips.

It's important to know, as you delve into Sinaee's selections for this year's anthology, that this collection is meant to serve as a touchstone, a record, a reckoning. What are Canadian poets writing right now? What work by Canadian poets is making its way into journals, in print and online, both here in Canada and beyond our borders? And which poems, from among those offerings, do we feel compelled to gather and bring forward in this annual accounting? Each year, our guest editor combs through multiple editions of dozens of journals, seeking stand-out work from among their editors' selections. That editor changes annually for good reason: just as cadences and nuances of craft shift from year to year; and as the concerns of poets (and the journals that publish their work) evolve in response to what's going on around them; it's important that the anthology's eye on our poetry doesn't remain static either. As series editor, I stay put to welcome back our devoted readers, our poets and appreci-ators of poetry, our teachers and scholars, all those who care about the state of Canadian poetry, who've hitched themselves to this ancient craft—and also, I hope, to usher in new readers. I recruit and work closely with our guest editors, but they're the ones who venture deep into the wilds of the year in poetry and bring back what was there, waiting to be found.

*

When we emerged from the escape room, we felt strangely elated. Refreshed. For a short time, we'd been absorbed in an otherworld. Though we were fully engaged in the experience, we were also outside ourselves—we'd escaped. But the escape was *out* of the ordinary world—out of the perpetual problem of our own selves—and *into* the imaginary room, not the other way around. While there, we could inhabit, and on some level observe, the versions of ourselves that came to life in that altered existence, that rose to meet it.

In her essay "What Does Poetry Do?" from her collection *Experiments in Distant Influence*, Nova Scotia author Anne Simpson writes about what's possible when we give ourselves up to the mechanisms of poetry. She uses the experience of reading one's way through the brutal wars of the *Iliad* to illustrate poetry's effects: "It is not just that after reading Homer's *Iliad* we feel as though we've been hauled through the burning lands, the ash lands. We haven't just witnessed war; we've participated in it. It's not simply a case that poetry, that all literature, allows us to be attentive to otherness, to imagine otherness, it is that we enter a world of otherness."

In that otherness, we see ourselves. That, writes Simpson, is the alternative offered by poetry: "the ability to see oneself," which is "the beginning of knowing and mastering oneself—the beginning of wisdom." This leads to the chance, by no means guaranteed, that we might "awaken from the dream of ourselves."

Poetry is neither a trap nor a puzzle, and not every poem is all-consuming and urgent. But there's no mistaking that, when you dare to step into the world of a poem—a successfully executed poem, I mean—from the first line, you are hit full-force by the poem's sensory cues. You have entered an environment of the poet's own making, and in that place, you become fully awake. Or *differently* awake. Awake to the unfamiliar airiness or stuffiness of the poem's "rooms," and the light therein. When I enter the strange and only partly knowable place of a poem, I grow tense and alert (as we did in the escape room). I watch myself take the poem in. I let it do its work on me. Who am I, in this space? Is this, finally, the real me, coming to the fore?

Within any given poem lies no clear mystery a reader can solve. They're engaged, after all, with a poem, not a riddle. (Poem riddles do exist, but they're a rarity these days.) For those who give themselves over to the poem's rhythms and sounds, its sights and textures and smells—and to the feelings those cues evoke—there are sure to be moments of recognition that land like soft explosions within, the aftermath of which is often an aura of relief, a potent sense of not being alone in this world. (This, in part, is what Sinaee means by poems making things "real.") But no triumphant "oh, I get it!" awaits at the end, no code that will, at last, open, with a satisfying click, the heavy padlock on the magic shop's door latch—nothing that will render the poem, and the effect it had, explainable in simple terms. That's because poems aren't for solving; they're for getting lost inside.

Still, there's something about being caught up in these words that have obviously been chosen just so, and following along these lines that have a maddening way of bending, falling off, or turning back on themselves, that is awfully *like* being caught up in a deliberately constructed enigma. Something is expected of you here, that much is clear. But what? The thrill of the escape room is not only in finding the answer, though there is satisfaction in that, for sure. It's in the search. The thrill of poetry is in realizing the search—one you hadn't even known you needed to embark on—has begun. This is a quest for what, you ask? If we could answer that, we wouldn't need poems at all. In *The Hatred of Poetry*, Ben Lerner writes, "Poetry becomes a word for an outside that poems cannot bring about, but can make felt, albeit as an absence …"

You read, you pause, you go back to the beginning to start reading again. You have a sneaking suspicion that the poet, who knows the way out, won't make it easy to find.

Anita Lahey
Ottawa, Ontario, unceded Algonquin,
Anishinabek territory
May 2023

Bardia Sinaee

INTRODUCTION

The Poet's Job: Keeping It Real in the Age of Synthetic Text

Too many best-of anthologies hedge their bets. Some people feel that it is categorically impossible, even absurd, to select the best examples of a given art form in a given period and appoint them duly, as if poems could be weighed and judged like pumpkins at a harvest fair. Without doubting the sincerity of their convictions, I am happy to report that the critics are wrong, for I have selected the fifty best Canadian poems of the year.

Superlatives like "best" are meaningless without parameters, and parameters arise from objectives. What is the best vehicle? It depends on your goal. If you want to haul lumber, the best vehicle is a truck. If you want to die, opt for a motorcycle. So, what are the fifty best poems? It depends on another question: What are poems *for*? Together, the pieces in this anthology constitute an answer.

"Give me a winch poem to unspool the infinite turban / of brain fog; a turbine poem to ventilate those trees in my lung forest," writes Tolu Oloruntoba in "Heel Poem / Black-Hooded." Here is a poet with purpose, bossing the poem around like a hired goon. "I want this depression pissing blood," he writes. "I want renal-stone poems that never let go of corridors, / stabbing from within with boot knives." With sadistic pleasure and anatomical precision, he inflicts the pain of depression back onto itself. The poem gives depression a body, then bashes its kidneys with a sock full of pennies "to allow it to die like the rest of us." Oloruntoba conjoins his gory scenes with semicolons, denying us the reprieve of a full stop, until we finally glimpse the sun and begin to breathe again. The poem makes depression *real*. To me, this is what poems are for: making things real.

Language does more than communicate information from person to person; it intermediates between ideas and reality. Many of the best Canadian poems of the year consciously play in this space.

John Steffler's "Unwelcome Scene" opens with an admonition: "There's no use telling yourself be careful / what you dread." A series of dreadful thoughts ensues: dark ocean swells, scorched landscapes, a shrill parade during which "no one will look at you alone on the sidewalk." Here, the poem pivots, contrasting the baroque nightmares with the stark simplicity of a seemingly real horror: standing on the sidewalk, alone and unnoticed, as the love of your life walks by arm in arm with someone else, looking "buoyant" (that is, unburdened by *you*). Then the poem seems to turn its attention completely toward the reader:

> ... It will come. What haunts you
> most. You attract it. Why do I feel it's
> the poet's job to say this? ...

How unnerving to be addressed so directly! Is this an observation or a warning? How do we attract what haunts us? Do not look to the poem for answers. Look within yourself. Poets do not know; they imagine. This poet dreads recklessly. With a handful of images and a forthright tone, he evokes the devastation and self-reflection of an ego-shattering moment, observes it from within, then steps outside to comment on it, to make friends with it (and art). Like many poets in this anthology, Steffler's command of language verges on alchemy.

Rhiannon Ng Cheng Hin's "Telephone Repairman" conjures a person from a tool. The speaker finds an old hammer on the ground on top of a hill and imagines becoming a telephone repairman, "a figure in faded linen / drifting from pole / to pole, tool box in hand." The imagery is murky, obscured by "summit haze" and "calving brume" through which the repairman drifts like a ghost, existing "as interstitial noise" amid the telephone signals. Contrary to its intended function, the hammer is described as "evidence of the intractable," of that which is not easily shaped. The tool is returning to its base elements, rusting in the tektite-strewn dirt (tektites are small glassy objects believed to have formed during meteorite impacts), and the speaker considers finding its dead owner's grave to "return it / to his earthen fist." Despite the title, this poem is driven by a destructive impulse. From their vantage on the summit, the poet gazes down on the technological artifice of the connected world, its "bleak signal lights" and "insufferable wires," and imagines tearing it down to bury it in "unanswerable peat," to make the world real again.

*

In November 2022, as I was busy reading poetry magazines for this anthology, OpenAI released a free research preview of Chat-

GPT, a "large language model" (LLM) that identifies patterns in a vast collection of data to teach itself how to generate human-like responses to user prompts—a prediction machine for language. The prediction power of artificial intelligence (AI) has already helped people map protein structures and coordinate planetary defence. It outperforms humans in the analysis of medical imaging. The efficiency and purported objectivity of algorithms also mean AI will be increasingly relied upon to prop up overburdened social systems and institutions facing a crisis of legitimacy (hence the dystopian horror of "predictive policing"). AI's potential impact on humanity has been compared to that of electricity. Now, it is creating images, stories, and poems on an unprecedented scale.

I will spare you a recap of all the AI-generated content that has since made the rounds. Some of it is fascinating. Unfortunately, a lot of the poetry sounds like this:

A cup of tea, a sunny day,
A friendly chat, a child's play.
These little things we take for granted,
Are the ones that make life enchanted.
   (from "Everyday Moments" by ChatGPT)

Most AI poetry is a series of insipid clichés arranged in rhyming quatrains. This is not ChatGPT's fault. Its job is to guess the next word based on the patterns it has picked up from processing web content, and the example above is a fair imitation of poetry on the internet. If a language model trained itself exclusively on datasets of carefully curated poetry—if the LLM got an MFA—it might generate less predictable language, but it is not clear what we would do with that. Reduce the poetry shortage? This brings us back to the question of what poetry is for.

Poets should not be threatened by the fact that every person with internet access can now create the poetic equivalent of hotel art. Although it involves technique, poetry is not a technical problem. We write it because we want to, not because we lack technology that can do it for us. Nor is poetry a zero-sum endeavour. Even if ChatGPT wrote better poems than we ever could, we would still write poetry, because there is more to writing than generating text. I write poetry for the same reason other people dance: because it is fun and probably good for my heart. Great poems, like the ones in this anthology, offer a recognition and mutual understanding I have not experienced outside of intimate conversation, and I write poetry because there is pleasure, value, and meaning in sharing this connection with others. I would not ask a robot to write my poems just as I would not ask it to hang out with my friends or savour my food. So, AI will not take the poet's job, but it will change it.

In March 2021, researchers at Google published a paper titled "On the Dangers of Stochastic Parrots," which noted the significant risks associated with "synthetic but seemingly coherent text" entering the discourse without any accountable author. We are entering an age in which much of what we read day to day will be created by agents that lack the capacity to *mean*. Meaning consists of more than the interpretation of symbols, according to the sociologist Neil Postman. "Meaning also includes those things we call feelings, experiences, and sensations that do not have to be, and sometimes cannot be, put into symbols." At its core, artificial intelligence is pure symbol, a vast string of binary code. Our feelings, experiences, and physical sensations are continuous and multifaceted, so when we express them using discrete values (words, binary), something is lost. Symbols cannot fully express the richness and range of human feeling and experience. Fortunately, every human reader also brings a lifetime of feelings, sensations, and associations to the table, which enables poetry to evoke introspection beyond what can be captured by symbols. Thus, a poem amounts to more than the sum of its words. In contrast, a large language model that has processed every bit of writing ever created cannot be moved by the words because it has no feeling or physical experience to draw upon; it can only engage with poetry as symbols representing instructions, a series of ones and zeros corresponding to electrical currents that are either on or off. This is why ChatGPT cannot *mean* as humans do. Any meaning it generates is ontologically synthetic. Ground beef.

Nevertheless, the text AI generates is meaningful to us. We may interact with it unknowingly and assume it is human. It may one day generate poetry that moves us to tears. Coming to terms with this requires a conceptual shift. AI cannot *become* intelligent so long as our idea of intelligence is rooted in human experience. Instead, our idea of intelligence will become more artificial. The metaphors we use to understand technology and humanity work both ways. When we speak of "processing" experiences, for example, we conceive of experience as information that can be integrated through a set of procedures, which makes the self a sort of central processing unit. "To discover truth," writes Meghan O'Gieblyn in *God, Human, Animal, Machine*, "it is necessary to work within the metaphors of our time, which are for the most part technological." Conceptually, the humanization of machines follows more than a century of the mechanization of humans, from the nineteenth-century principles of scientific management that segmented human work into a series of optimizable processes, to the assembly lines and mind-control experiments of the twentieth century, to the modern-day conception of the brain as a supercomputer that can be hacked and rewired. The latest manifestation of this trend was encapsulated by Sam Altman, CEO of OpenAI (the company behind ChatGPT), who tweeted on December 4, 2022, "i am a stochastic parrot, and so r u." If prediction machines can write our cover letters, help us come up with ideas, and seemingly relate to us, then maybe we are prediction machines.

I wrote earlier that language intermediates between ideas and reality, but if software applications with no ideas and no sense of reality can produce coherent language, then my anthropocentric understanding of language must change. As Maggie Nelson wrote in *The Argonauts*, "Words change depending on who speaks them; there is no cure."

There was a time when poetry did not exist outside of the human voice. It could not be recorded or otherwise converted into a system of symbols beyond speech. Anyone who recited poetry essentially gave life to it, but the work was not attributed to an individual author. Poetry changed with the written word. It changed again after the printing press mechanized the reproduction of writing. Now, AI is mechanizing writing itself. It remains to be seen exactly how this will change poetry, but it undoubtedly will.

Therefore, the pieces collected in this anthology constitute a historical snapshot of an idea of poetry, a collective articulation of what poems are for circa 2023. Animated by the desire, joy, wonder, humour, fear, grief, and doubt that make us real, these poems are our best expressions of humanity in a year of change for what it means to be human. So read them closely and keep them close by, in case you need a reminder.

Bardia Sinaee
Ottawa, Ontario, unceded Algonquin,
Anishinabek territory
April 2023

Sarah Yi-Mei Tsiang

THE AIR, THEN

I am 100 years pregnant, old as a tree
that must pry up its roots
to wade through the swamp-air.

It is the Year of the Rat,
and you, fetal, are curled and pink
inside the shredded nest of my womb

The world is a heaped pile
of broken trinkets and sharp edges.
The ether is a living virus

we breathe in sips. I want you to know
that when you were conceived
we shared air like water,

dipping our faces
in its cold pure sweetness.

—from *The Malahat Review*

Carolyn Smart

ASHES

(for Steffen, Nicholas and Daniel)

They handed me his ashes in what might have been
a shopping bag, with handles. Inside it was a cardboard box
and inside that, ashes in a see-through plastic bag.
The bag of ashes is heavy in my arms and shifts when pressed.
They're brown or beige like suede, a coverlet, a kitchen door.
I see the flecks of bone in ash the way I know late snowflakes
glow upon the soil. When we are ready, we stand together
in the field he loved so well to pour him on the ground,
around the trees and shrubs he tended over years,
the place his friends would play the games they loved.
I watch the bone chips lying on the soil like flakes of snow,
I see them lasting through the days of rain and wind,
the endless shaking of my heart. The bone chips do not fade.
Then one night after heavy storms, they disappear.
Like he did. But unlike him, I know that they're still there.

—from *Grain*

Nicholas Bradley

ATMOSPHERIC RIVER

Dear Kit: You said the storms taught you something
new, a weather term you hadn't known. Well, you
and grim me and everybody else. What's
a pedant to do but consult the good book?
The dictionary swings and whiffs. Phrases:
none. Etymologies: none. Definitions:
none. Quotations: none. Full text? Take
a wild guess. I look at these sweet nothings
through my own zeros, leer at drone footage
of the crumbled Coquihalla Highway
and the streaming porn of liquefied cities.
Above my mask I'm always fogged. Water,
water, everywhere. You tell me it's drier
than normal on your side of the Rockies.
The rain got stuck in traffic. I know the Bow
a little, Elbow too, and my lips are cracked
on your behalf. I dreamed I was an ocean
and woke up soaked and coughing, bedclothes
a lake. Aren't all rivers atmospheric?
That's why we love them, breathe them through our gills
and taste them with our feet. The skylight's drumming.
When this cold breaks I'll write some more. Till then
I dispatch your rightful precipitation
and all my best from this drenched island. Nick.

—from *Grain*

Luke Hathaway

BALLAD

after David Thomson

I was well past child-bearing years
and children had, though only three,
when I was walking on the strand
and a sea-grey selkie said to me,

> *O come away, my beautiful one,*
> *arise and come away with me.*
> *I am a man upon the land,*
> *I am a selkie in the sea.*

O how can I away with you?
A man I have, and children three.
If you had come when I was young
I would have gone away with thee.

> And home I went to my husband true
> and bounced my babies on my knee,
> but my dreams were full of the selkie's song,
> and the *Eli, Eli* of the sea.

So I went down to the shore again
and said, *All right, I'll go with thee:*
come up and claim what is thine own.
No answer came from the seal-grey sea.

So I went home to my husband true
and sang to my beautiful children three,
I am a woman on the land,
I am a selkie in the sea.

O come away, my beautiful one.
O why hast thou forsaken me?

—from *The Walrus*

David Barrick

BOB ROSS BEATS THE DEVIL

out of that brush. Wet on wet,
fingers rinsed and lemon-
fresh, keeping smudges off
the skyline. I'd like

that mellow voice to narrate
my taxes, navigate these bills.
The cat needs dental work again,
non-deductible. Bob rescued

squirrels and raccoons, let birds
land in his hair. Assembled
a backyard sanctuary. Snuffed
out the hell-spark of moods

in a thirty-minute landscape
blooming from ashtray to Eden.
I take a break and binge Netflix,
his risky brush strokes:

I'm sure he's ruined it each time
he adds another long black line
that morphs into a crisp pine. Mountain
peaks receding as the forest grows

lush, impasto-thick, and then a log cabin
that has no windows
                    but might soon.

                                        —from *Grain*

Olajide Salawu

A CARTOGRAPHER MAPS HIS WAY
OUT OF HIS COUNTRY

After Kei Miller

A cartographer talk say his country na sufferhead and
maps the sea as an alternative bridge. By that, I mean the
cartographer dreams of leaving the *trenches*. The
cartographer recounts how Chibok falls into rubble, how
women of Baga are led into the dark corridors by
shadows of strangers, how Odi falls on its feet and
children cannot lift themselves out of its ruins. The
cartographer talk say Aso Rock is the kingdom where
God and the twenty-four elders keep the altar clean. He says
across the street today, there is the gut of a woman on
the floor and a soldier holds a man by his neck and
screams at him, *guess where dead people go*! The
cartographer mumbles that the river is a huge jar of tears,
and the government advises there is no need for us to
think of water. He says it is hard to map your way out
for freedom in a country that says this is not your
Babylon. The cartographer says exile is also a famished
road even when you survive the sea.

—from *Grain*

Elana Wolff

CONCERN FOR SOUL CONSUMES ME

In the northern garden
dwell two tall
catalpa trees.
Their large and heart-
shaped pointy leaves, downy
undersides—soft as fontanelles.
They've let the spotted
red-capped woodpecker in.

Form is the polar opposite of chaos,
wrote Roberto B.
I take release from this and that

the dead, he said, yes even *the dead*
are being developed.
Eventually, by this conception, everyone
will be among the co-
developed dead.

Concern for soul consumes me.
I sit in the northern garden—
in the hazy
shady shape of it
and follow my steady breath—born
as it's being breathed, it seems. Streaming

so organically,
it can't be pre-constructed.

Invisible and thin and free,
as baffling as Kafka—
whose rendering of difficult things
was easier for him, it seems to me,
than birthing breath.
      Will teachers of any persuasion contravene me?

Not the two catalpa trees.
Not the spotted woodpecker. Not his crimson cap.

—from *Literary Review of Canada*

James Warner

DAME PHILOSOPHY

Anicius Boethius wrote *De consolatione*
in prison, charged with conspiracy.
It's thought that he was executed not long after,
in Pavia, place of his exile,
circa 524 CE.

As for the book, surely worth reading—
esteemed 'The Golden Volume' for centuries.
But then, who has the time?
Last night again trying to get through it
I fell asleep on the couch.

Deep, in the badly lit but great near-after,
taking shape, her form
emerging from the cursive gloom
as from eternity's cabinet ...
it was she, to the life, unchanged.

I woke, partly, in a crowd
of mute people packed into a dirigible
flying past a corner of the moon.
Solemnly deploying instruments
and occupied at monitors and charts,

all there seemed intent
on some far threshold. While astern
the earth veered slowly away
shrinking to the size of a robin's egg,
a marble. Gazing after it

with the ache one knows running
through an airport as the last flight departs,
I reached out. The dream broke.
And there I was, in the dead of night,
nodding over *De consolatione*.

—from *EVENT*

Robert Hogg

DEATH IS

a shift of
the centre

into darkness
a new point

of light
become real

—from *EVENT*

Erin McGregor

A EULOGY

spring, before the lilacs
but after the cherry
blossoms
C in the hospital and I am writing
a eulogy, I write it

in my head, while I sleep,
in the shower,
while I eat. I write it
through my windshield at red

lights. it shadows my eyes, notices
small things. look, it says:
a hawk on a sign post.
the sun is diffuse

all the way to the hospital the impending
moment
buzzes and burrs
like a wasp trapped.

his hand reaches, his grip still
strong he is open, a Madonna lily.
oh, he says, oh,
over and over, surprised.

and all the words
gathered so carefully, these
impotent, conceited
things
evaporate like breath.

—from *The Antigonish Review*

Alison Braid

FEAR OF DESIRE

Just this morning Julia
scraped frost from the swingset
into my mittened hands, saying, *Snow*,
the word from that morning's flashcard
with its perfect cool geometry,
and waited for me to toss it up,
make it fall down as snow,
as it never had before.
She's performing a miracle, you tell Julia,
though we are all outside of language
and understanding, only the miracle
joyous between us, not needing
our thought or description.

Leaving work, we stop in the underpass
where carp are swimming,
thick bodies flickering in deep
green buckets. In two weeks
it's Christmas. Soft round mouths
leap towards the hose's freshwater.
My face becomes the blank moon
of the underpass spilling over them.
You point, choosing your fish,
and a man leans forward with a flashing knife,
with an apron stiff with blood.

The carp is luminous, white
and pearled as rice. Our desires
surface and show their bright
underbellies. First want
is the method, then we are.
Lightly, it begins to snow.

—from PRISM *international*

Michael Ondaatje

5 A.M.

For Stan Dragland and for Kris Coleman

The wilderness of our youth, an empty barn,
dancing with friends into the small hours,
then daylight and the cars swerving away
wordless into the dawn

It arrives all at once tonight,
not as memory, but as a gift
from forgetfulness,
as a desire can wake you

or this poem
based on the accidental change of speed
in a friend's camera into slow motion

So now I remember
the rest of our shadows
as we danced, all our heartbeats
under the thunder

and I can speak to you the way
we once sang farewells out of our cars
late at night, when those
goodbyes remembered everything

—from *Brick*

Joanna Streetly

GYRE

I did have stepsons. No, I should say I *do*.
And I did look for them, but I should say I didn't
find them. No one found them. I should say that

my stepsons were not found, unless you count
those few bones, that tattered shirt, the Levi's that lasted
all those months in the kelp. And did you know

that kelp beds—the kind that are impossible
to propel your kayak over, or through, the kind
that make a carpet on the sea, one that makes you believe

you can walk on water—did you know
that those kelp beds are keepers? Whole collections:
white Styrofoam dots; water, half-drunk, in plastic

bottles with blue labels and blue lids; sleeping sea otters,
sometimes more than one; half-shells of mussels, floating
like blue Venetian gondolas

in circular canals with no exits; tiny minnows that leap
for no reason and land, not in water, but on blades of kelp,
some ridged, some smooth, all of them

growing before your sunlit eyes, while the minnows
in their silver straitjackets jerk and gasp. Deeps and shallows.
These bones once danced the deer dance

played at stepping through water
with exaggerated slowness: (Blue heron.
O great one! Your disapproving side-eye.)

Catch-me-if-you-can: a cormorant diving,
flash of dark motion. Not a hand waving. Paddle further.
Crab float, orange and black. Not a life jacket.

Eyes becoming tunnels. Arms becoming wood. Legs becoming
sea through the hull of my kayak. Slippery boys becoming fish,
becoming deer, becoming clouds.

Every time I look they are somewhere else
and me? the last to spot them. I dredge pop-eyed dreams,
distended song bladders. And I should say that nothing

is the past. I should say that I search circular canals with no exits
knowing I do have stepsons. I do. Nothing is the past.
They are there in my ribcage. Knocking.

—from *Prairie Fire*

Allan Serafino

HARE

A white hare has been living in my backyard all winter
in his home in the cave under the fir tree.

He thumps the snow from his feet against the house
perhaps just to sound his hundred names.

The imprint of those feet is white on white,
small scrim and blush on the snow and a prophecy

of seedlings under the tree are also all we know of him.
Everywhere that winter there were rumours

small reports and the sky heavy with doubt.
Clear doubt.

—from *The New Quarterly*

Sarah Lachmansingh

HE HASN'T ARRIVED AND SOMEONE HAS TURNED ON THE STREETLAMPS

my mother inhales mouthfuls
of her own hair, her salad

fork still clasped in her fist.
she could prong it through her romaine

or my wrist if she woke, dazed,
but she'd have wished it were his face.

she sleeps over her own plate
of meat as i imagine my skin dimpled

with four neat dots, as i imagine my forgiveness,
ripe in my mouth, saying,

i am your daughter, i am
your daughter, as i imagine

the light behind her bruise
with a shadow

i mistake for his body.

—from *EVENT*

C.P. Cavafy, translated by Evan Jones

HE PLANNED TO READ

He planned to read. Two or three books
lie open beside him: historians, poets.
But he read for just ten minutes
and gave up, dozing off
on the sofa. Books are his obsession,
but he's twenty-three and very pretty
and this afternoon longing passed through
his tender skin, his lips. The fire
of longing passed through his beautiful skin—
without any guilt as to the cause of that fire.

—from *Exile Quarterly*

Matt Rader

HEAT DOME

We swam in the lake at 10 a.m.
before it grew too hot,
the five of us—
two divorced parents,
our teenagers, my mother—
at the little public access
where the neighbour with the tennis courts
has a lakeside infinity pool.
I've a spider bite
on my hip
the exact pinks of the wildfire
smoke-filtered
sunlight. In Similkameen and Osoyoos and Penticton,
the ashes of Catholic churches
can't cool.
Spider-bite-sky.
Rashy light.
In Xanadu, did Kubla Khan
A stately pleasure-dome decree,
is what I remember
most vividly from Grade 12 poetry.
Infinity is when it never ends. We swam out
to the nearest buoy,
a white and pink ball on the surface
of the lake. We followed its shadowy chain down

to a shadowy slab of concrete
in the milfoil at 15 feet
What is pleasure
without an ending. When the spider bit me
I didn't feel anything. Back on the beach
on our slip of public property,
beneath a bower of maple trees
we were cool. How could we be
happy, we asked,
but we were
happy. The spider bite had its own source
of heat. It was something
inside me.

—from *EVENT*

Tolu Oloruntoba

HEEL POEM / BLACK-HOODED

Like the mice of my childhood, blowing to soothe heels they
      nibbled on
with white chainsaw teeth, this mood settles like 40 stories of
      smog,
floating before the building of carbon climbs my breath, the
      hand
at my chest clutching for purchase crushed, too, thoughts of
      escape squirming
in the Brownian chamber. Give me a winch poem to unspool
      the infinite turban
of brain fog; a turbine poem to ventilate those trees in my lung
      forest,
the ones with elastic bands of sap garroting their craning
      necks; I want a crane poem to
deconstruct the sarcophagus-heavy helmet, and corset, the
      luminescent poster-sun on the wall;
a wrecking ball poem I can hide inside—a knuckle duster
that breaks the warden's eye-socket, enjambs the signet finger
      in a door;
a sock poem with pennies for the kidneys of this alley—I want
      this depression pissing blood
after hits to the side; I want renal-stone poems that never let go
      of corridors,
stabbing from within with boot knives; a heel poem to with-
      stand jeers and be foul,

fight dirty against the adulation of sadness; and take a windlass
    to its intestines;
I am advocating violence, a hand to wrench the lead apron
from the gonads of this thing, allow it to die like the rest of us,
but not before we all get a glimpse of sun.

—from *The Walrus*

Peter Norman

THE HOLLOWING

The fretboard of a hundred-year-old lute.
Shelves of books choked up with knowledge
and with gnawing blackhead
book lice turning knowledge
into fecal specks. Felled heaps
of magazines—hunting, hot rods,
politics, pornography—some bleached
by daylight after years on the same sill.
Used rags. Unopened sets of dishes.
Flea market acquisitions in a box
alive with fleas. Brand-new packs of collars
meant to keep the fleas from pets. Just anything,

in fact, he came across or scavenged from the trash
or found at prices no one could refuse. Refuse
rubbing shoulders with the shining plunder
from the dollar store. Rotting meats
chockablock inside a disconnected freezer.
Insecticide and bugs enough to eat the factory
insecticides are brewed in. Bolted ceiling racks
in every room, all garlanded
with pots and mugs and coats and lengths of rope
knotted up, festooned with flags of ribbon.
A pyramid of used and wadded toilet tissue
self-erecting in the mouldy tub.

Oven jammed with pots and plates
and liquefying foods alike. Rat traps
sprung, still clutching vertebrae.
You get the gist. We had to make our path
by plucking items out of it, a sculptor's
practice, kind of. We had to keep an eye,
we thought at first, for items we could sell, ensure
no chance at recompense went missed.
We soon dismissed those thoughts.
Wasn't worth the sift, the lift, the gagging
revelation. Better simply shovel stuff
into the bins, and damn the best of it.

Trucks came and went with Dumpsters on their backs.
We shovelled till the light was gone. There was a place
to sit, but only one: a lonely chair
at a bare spot on the table; half a foot away,
a tubby old TV. Six pairs of rabbit ears.
We sat, you on my lap, and breathed the teeming air.
You wanted out of there. Me too.
But with a week till sell date, cleaners booked and queued
but none prepared to tackle this first purge,
we had to get to work. "Sorry," I said,
to you, for me, for who I'm from. My own inherent filth.
My cumulation growing, sprawling. All the all of me.

—from *The New Quarterly*

Seth MacGregor

HOUSE FIRE ON COOK ROAD

Bong in the armoire, on the floor a caved-in steel guitar,
an unmarked urn in the corner above the cupboards
above the piles of ash, wet drywall, glass that we're
shoving into buckets and bags. We're wearing dust
masks and "Stutters" shirts. Scott Stone, curlicue
moustache, the project manager's assistant, the parvenu,
tells me to go downstairs. To cozen? Howbeit,
I slug my weight in ash bags to the garbage pit.
I'm eighteen and I get to hit some walls
with a sledgehammer. Then I'm given a drill, "you
take out the screws." The bookshelf I unscrew
from a wall in the basement is peeled off its caulk
revealing a small room with no light fixtures,
a heat lamp and a shower drain. We all take pictures.

—from *Grain*

John Elizabeth Stintzi

I LEFT THE BOY FOREVER

I left the boy forever
once, climbing
out the throat of *him*.

For a time after I perched
upon his shoulder.
For a time (until *forever*)

I let people see us together—
as *one* simply divided
like a globe by its parallels.

But how harsh the parallax.
How long the driveway.
How firmly the Loctite

held the cold bolt of me
into *his* coarse threads.
As my dad taught me,

crouched in a tractor's gut
with propane and ratchet,
to remove myself from *him*

I applied heat to stubbornness.
Immolated my tattered self
like a self-suffocating field.

Like the time my dad wired
the flaming, oil-soaked rag
to the rear of his quad

and drove it out across
the pasture, engulfing,
I am far more fertile now.

Air reaches soil.
Coaled turf rots into life.
New green retakes the canvas.

I left the boy forever once.
But I'm ever dragged back
through the gaze of the world.

Every morning I must rise
to the warm light
of *his* burning.

—from *The Ex-Puritan*

Misha Solomon

I'M A HOLE / I'M A POLE / MY GREAT-GRANDMOTHER WAS A POLE

my eyes are holes / my pores are holes / my asshole is a hole
my arms are poles / my toes are poles / my nose is a pole with
    two holes
my great-grandmother left Poland in 1920-something / my
    great-grandmother was three years old / my great-grand-
    mother always said she was born in Warsaw but we know
    that was a lie it was some shtetl

my mouth is a hole / my ears are holes / I'd die if you added
    another big enough hole
my fingers are poles / my legs are poles / yes fine my cock is a
    pole with one hole
my great-grandmother owned a dress shop / my great-grand-
    mother would have died in Poland / my
    great-grandmother died here and I've never been to
    Poland

my want is a hole / my need is a hole / my therapy is a hole dis-
    guised as a pole
my nipples are poles in the cold / my love is a pole and a hole /
    sometimes I can be the perfect pole
my great-grandmother had holes and poles / my great-grand-
    mother's parents had holes and poles / I wonder if during
    a transatlantic escape from pogroms and their ilk my

great-grandmother's parents' holes were so deep there was
relief to be found in seeing them inversely / that is as poles

—from *The /tɛmz/ Review*

Joel Robert Ferguson

from LAST THINGS LASTING

(2)

Enhazed magenta sun rises on the eastern prayer; he sets
baleful in Wawa, fourteen hours on. So much. Signage: *GOD IS
WATCHING YOU.* Disaster on the tarmac. Braintree Avenue.
Detox Crunch Salad. Old Woman Bay Scenic Tour. Burn out, yr

name is burnt out gratfitto'd lakeshore husks. Mythic a nightmare
of course to live within. Sky burial makes a comeback. Make
a list of celebrities and snacks as eastward the wagons.

Senescence drops the mission, the call, the body. Somehow,
carved into public stall wall of Marathon, Ontario's
one mall, "Vercingeotrix" (sic). Like Little Italy-bound
once youngling, I was drawn on as if by an electric rail

a light tugging forward on my head toward quest
ions about the multiplicity of signs, their RO
obscurely linked at the abandoned farm to novel mansion

ratio. "This is a sacred place" [Kleinzahler], it is God's country, don't
you see? Signs proclaim it so along the 17, in case
the traveller's eye remains influent in Ottawa River valley...
Re: turn the soil or run to ground, beauty is signified by the buying

up of rural poverty by the Wes Anderson hinterland.
Cottage. Outpost. Neither your home. "They won't stop swearing" or
"they kill our children in the street and hide behind their MRAPS".

Rue Colony Street. A little push, then away. Propel beyond
means of transfer. Idle by the hard hats past points of reference.
Long distance cyclist passing Nipigon, what is your function?

—from *Qwerty*

James Scoles

LAST TRAIN HOME

I'm buzzing with the energy of a
dying florescent tube as two lovers
duck out of our car just before the

doors shut & make for a nearby
love hotel. Tomorrow I will teach
pharmaceutical executives how to

present their unpleasant research
in the most pleasing way. Much as
I want my night to whirl into more

madness & wake in a whole new
world without worry, my little tin
earthquake shack waits for me &

my disaster to wrestle into & through
another night of little sleep, sweat &
dreams tethered to my walls & caged

in me like my clients' many research
animals—cows & monkeys, mostly.
Some kidneys & livers can only handle

so much & you simply have to see.
Four deaths out of a thousand is great news,
my client told me. They test hundreds

of cows before pressing on to monkeys.
My tour of the facility lasted exactly five
minutes & left me soaking in this alcoholic

dream for days, nights & not happily ever
after. Somewhere between the acidic taste
& smell of death & the bittersweet sound

of pain singing, I passed out, into the arms
of two clients. They carried me outside, into
the wet Tokyo air. Told me the animals are

well-cared for. They showed me shrines
built for research animal spirits & now
I dream of cartoon cows & monkeys

all making their flight arrangements
to those wide-open & golden, well-
fenced fields in the sky.

—from *Grain*

Louise Carson

LITTLE FIRES

Even after
long time gone,
there are small attachments,
little fires and obligations,
conflagrations,
drowning time.

Dibble, dibble, dirk.
Enjoy the burning colours,
the diseased mind
at work.

—from *The Nashwaak Review*

Susan Gillis

MOVING DAY

Hilltop, apple tree, broken
bench, damn you, weather, damn you

bears, damn the whole wide ringing
valley. My lost toboggan

staves and splinters through dry grass.
Shredded baseboards I will my father

entering institutional limbo
not to see.

I wheel him in a chair
through the blue kitchen (big

prep, big storage, big cold, he wants
to see everything, why am I afraid?)

into the private garden. *I don't suppose*
that gate's supposed to be unlatched like that—

We stare for a minute through the crack.

You might just pull that—
I smooth the shawl over his shoulder.

I could open the door.

We stare at the sliver of traffic and time.

—from *Grain*

Hilary Clark

from MY MUTED YEAR

02/03/2020

Crocuses, violet frost. The morning census of the dead. I need a
carwash for my brain, as when suds rise and smother the car
windows and then the rinse clicks in and then the dryer. Briefly
a face among the lines of fleeing water beads. Furrows on your
cheek? Wear a mud or kelp mask. You're a sloth, you'll never
finish first. What miserly odds attended your birth? What trucu-
lent fairy?

03/23/2020

Purell or bleach? Sanitize nerves on the hour. Locked-down
aquarium: stingrays, jellyfish swim in sad blue light. For divina-
tion, consult swallows and butterflies, alder and ash. And
monkeys. You there, stop playing the mantic poet while the
dying heave in their oxygen capsules, seeing stars. Lo, the great
nebula Nescience. What was the question?

04/07/2020

A microdose of psilocybin in my coffee, CBD drops in my tea. An hour of soulful breathing a day, then a punch at the rising sticky dough of hopelessness. What miserly odds? That's me walking my hunched shadow along a wall of pink puffy graffiti. Neon bardo fireworks—fluorescence is the state I seek. Used needles, condoms underfoot.

05/15/2020

Moon men stack coffins three to five high. Wild goats roam the streets: briefly a god's head, chewing violets. Constellations of cold stars mark your late style. Just put on your lateral-thinking cap, associations are free. Yes, glibness was ever the clever monkey riding you. Black body bags for mendicants. Burned spoons.

—from *Grain*

Sue Sinclair

THE NASHWAAK RIVER

The Sisson mine project is a proposal to build one of the world's largest open-pit mines for tungsten and molybdenum in the heart of the upper Nashwaak River, near the village of Stanley.

The river: it used to feel unstoppable.

What is beauty without the rush of blood, the promise it used to evoke?

"[T]he possibility of a structural failure of a TSF embankment is so unlikely that it cannot reasonably be considered a credible accident or malfunction, and is thus not considered further in this EIA Report."*

Thistles glint, molybdenum-like. Wild strawberries dangle from delicate trusses.

The water is bright as an eye; I feel like I could look into it and it would know what I know about the Feds, the arsenic, the fluoride.

A middle-aged woman in flaw-concealing black swimsuit and white bathing cap wades up to her waist from the far bank.

Is there really such a thing as a core of self that can't be harmed, broken, broken into?

Uncannily calm, the flickering current.

Uncannily calm the ox-eyes, the vervain, the nightshade.

I consider the possibility of structural failure.

A credible accident: the damselfly perched on a stalk of timothy grass, shaggy with seed.

Before my eyes, beauty concedes, becomes a tactic, putting off the inevitable.

At the foot of the maple a cluster of white *Peiris* butterflies sucks the salt from a patch of dog pee.

Come live with me and be my love …

The firs blink their dusty lashes in disbelief.

—from *Prairie Fire*

* From the *Sisson Environmental Impact Assessment*

Meghan Kemp-Gee

A NEWLY DISCOVERED SPECIES
OF LIZARD WITH DISTINCTIVE
TRIANGULAR SCALES

I am Charles Darwin. I eat owlflesh at Cambridge University.
I have discovered something, an entirely new species
with tropical fever in its reptile fingers. I am busy
with taxonomying its most peculiar and three-sided
armour, its six-toed fitness for these latitudes and its perfect
speckled eggs like forlorn love notes, black mammalian eyes
    pinpricked
with blue as if caught in headlights suddenly. I've isolated
a cold-weathered ancestor in its DNA. I'm going to clone
its terrible antlered children, its swarming descendants,
    outsource
its coiled vertebrate progenitors to secret facilities
hungry for fresh IP. I've obtained Steven Spielberg to direct
the lizard's biography. I will name it after royalty. I am
deliriously pleased. I find myself full of discovery.
I am homesick, boat-sick. I am hotel-room-sick. I want to go
    home.

—from *Plenitude Magazine*

Rocco de Giacomo

NOT UNTIL IT DOES

A surgical intern is separating
a branch of the pulmonary artery
from a cancerous node when she brushes
too close, nicks an arterial wall and a river
issues forth, filling the ventral cavity
with blood at a rate of three litres
per minute, but what does
that mean? The body's purpose
is to keep things close enough
that they are indistinguishable
from ourselves, and we've undone that.
Forty light years to the diamond planet,
55 Cancri E, now seems reasonable
as things unravel; the orbit cuts close enough
to the host star that days
are filled with oceans of lava, and nights
are a glittering supercontinent, a sanguineous
crust we've forgotten about. Remember
we have to leave any jewellery at home
the day of the surgery. We wash and fast
and take all the precautions,
and wouldn't you know it, one slip
of the scalpel and we are on our way
to becoming an inland sea. If not
for the senior surgeon, who steps forward,

stops up the flood with his pinky finger, winks
and says well, you're in deep shit now,
aren't you?

—from *Prairie Fire*

Matthew King

ON THE DUCKS WHO ARE PEOPLE
AND THE DUCKS WHO ARE DUCKS

In the animated movie that's made for children
there is one particular duck who can talk and is
a person, while the rest of the ducks just quack and are
only ducks. If those ducks are shot they will die and you
can eat them, unlike Daffy Duck who is shot again
and again and his feathers are singed but he can't die.

The duck who talks and is a person is the one duck
who matters. That duck is you. You identify with
that duck, not the others, because you are a person,
a person who talks and matters and survives, unlike
the others, who quack and die and will be eaten or
whatever might happen to them—it doesn't matter.

But all the other people, it turns out, also feel
the same way about it: they also identify
with the only duck who can talk and is a person,
who gets things done in the world, whose life could be wasted,
but isn't. Know this: everyone alive is that duck.
Every single person is that cartoon character.

The ducks themselves, though, the actual ducks in the world,
the ducks who live in the water between ice and ice,
those ducks don't make distinctions between ducks who are ducks
and ducks who are people. None of them talk. None of them
want to. They all quack and they don't know why that matters.
This isn't to say they're not missing something. They are.

But we must not miss what they're not missing, in ourselves
or in them. They open onto the world like we do.
They are moved by the sun like we are, they feel it and
they awaken themselves. They are moved by hunger like
we are, feel their emptiness, seek to fill their bodies.
They are moved by the cold like we are, shiver, notice

their shivering and they fly until they've outflown it.
In the lengthening night, their world shrunken by darkness,
they push with their voices against its closing borders,
against the encroachment of known and unknown others.
Some are taken unseen in the dark and some are shot
after dawn, in the light of day, when the light goes out.

—from *Rust and Moth*

Beatriz Hausner

THE ORGASMS ROOM

One day the man she had invented for herself appeared on the doorstep of the house at Rue du Château. She had seen him in dreams, imagined his sex, its head, its dimensions. She had conjured the outward appearance of his skin; his fairness growing inward of its layers, the delicate lines that defined his upper and lower lips, the texture of his hair; the fact of his luminosity. These and other aspects, she kept in reserve to pleasure her mind. Time, life's complicated fabrics and the tight weave of her days had worked their hardness into forgetting, so that the ideal man she had so carefully pursued had faded into the deep recesses of her mind where he lived with her longing.

When he came, she recognized him immediately. His skin had darkened somewhat, for he had journeyed far in her absence, to places others would not dare venture. He had wrestled with women and men of formidable cruelty, translated his sufferings into old, perhaps dead languages, which he pronounced perfectly.

No sooner did his tongue touch hers than she understood that their paths mirrored each other, as though they had been drafted by the hand of an overseer, ensuring that their course was tortuous, that they meandered slowly and through deep crevasses of both anguish and joy.

—from *Exile Quarterly*

Joseph Kidney

OSCAIL DO BHÉAL

1.

My mother, by the orange snore
of the electric fireplace, is playing solitaire
on her iPad. She is always changing
the subject. *If the Catholics don't have time*
for women, I don't have time for the Catholics.
There is rain sizzling cold on the skylight
or squirrels, scarpering. Everyone's taking a turn
for the worse, and she follows their declines
with compassion, with curiosity,
and with curious compassion. Her drink
is water with a faint sting of lemon.

2.

In our home she was the farthest from home.
For others her accent had a snag and a warp
entirely hidden from my brother and me.
Maybe the voice they heard was an umbrella,
bad luck to open indoors, bad luck because
the people who raise a shelter within a shelter
have traded too much for caution. She sets out
a ramekin's worth of blueberries, humming
the carcass of a song picked clean by years

of remembering. I say I'll say a Hail Mary
for you. She says Enough of the stage Irish.

3.

She didn't forget the nuns of her childhood,
the *Deo gratias*, the *saecula saeculorum*,
but somewhere along the way she traded
religion for recycling, its weekly offices,
to separate the hard from the soft plastics
as one star differs from another star in glory.
Here, if anywhere, was the refutation
of use being our limit of involvement
in the world. The aseptic broth cartons,
their nacre-like inner foil, the bubble-lined
mailers, and discs of soiled cardboard cut
from boxes of takeaway. In the morning
they are like the grass that grows
to be mown and fragrant in the evening.

4.

And in the evenings she would help us
get ready for bed, saying *oscail do bhéal*
which meant (and still means) open your mouth.
And I opened my mouth, and she brushed
away with elbows and vigour, almost as if
she were cleaning a gutter. And later I lay
in the dark, scared to death and restlessness,

not by what couldn't and was
but by what wasn't and could.
And she would come and lie beside me
which, by simplifying, fortified—
a lull, a numbness, a lumen.
How I'm not quite sure. But it would seem
the point of lullabies,
to drop you off along the way
as they carry on to somewhere
else you cannot follow.

—from *Grain*

Jana Prikryl

OUR SECOND

A closed current
as small as a necklace
this water. Looking down at the pebble beach
from a window as tall as story. They'd done the tests
and only later I thought, nobody said
looks good. I don't mind losing the baby
our second, just interfere with the first.
But I was big and worried for myself. Pain or danger
and didn't want to see its face—I see it already—
made wrong by virus. Down there the pebble beach
our friends, comparing their finds, worried I'd solve this
the easy way, unaware one thing constantly
enters another, becoming not one with it
but taking its place, and on and on, a current

—from *The Walrus*

Anna Moore

PKOLS EQUINOX

A sand flea lives in bladder-wrack,
stinking copper drifts on the beach,
and knows neither pain nor cold.
Three little girls run headlong down to the water,
and stop. We've all been bitten.
They wade into the sea, and the earth creaks,
wishing it could stand as they stand—
arms out in glee, goosebumped.
Today there's no relief from the smog,
unless you're underwater or buried
in someone's arms.
The fleas are in their glory now,
pricking the atmosphere like needlepoint.
The sky bears down like an open palm.
The little girls' legs have turned red,
but they pay no heed; turn over
another crab-riddled rock.
To them a swathe of sea lettuce
is as beautiful as an evening gown.
What is time if not a void to fill
with anemones, rock fish, purple chitons?
Later the water will fling back its hair and retreat,
leaving the massy sand unprinted and alone.

—from *The Fiddlehead*

Meaghan Rondeau

PORTRAIT OF THE AUTHOR
FUCKING WITH LINEAR TIME
WHILE MAKING NO LOVE AT ALL

I might as well jump right in. "I have a date
on Tuesday," he says. If I stood up and flung myself from this—
this—I don't know what to call it, this
craggy warmthforsaken nightsoaked precipice,
there'd be nothing he could do
to save me. Too late.
"And another one on Friday." Too
dark. He'd never get to me, my body
broken on the rocks below or sunk into the ocean
further below, shocked frozen. Or both. Smash
and/or splash. "I'm excited."

Really, it's already too late. Way
too dark, too. I'm tired
of the new year. It started yesterday. So far
it's been all the same shit.
The starlight must be disgusted, having streaked
across the whole lonely universe to land
on the opposite of a date: a man and a woman
who took a path as far as it went
and ended up on the rocks
just past nightfall. Slumped on a boulder, I stare

into the slick deep glassdark of the Georgia Strait,
ass numb, mind stonecolder. I'm splitting

spacetime, emptying my self into places more hospitable
than *here* and *now*: into the light
across the water, Vancouver; into the warmth
of indoors, my apartment, the relief
of containment, walled solitude, the fat oval loaf
of cat drowsing at the end of the bed; into recollected
        fragments
of him and me animated, connected, contented, friends; into
        the day
far in the future when, at long friggin' last,
I start writing this poem.

                        Okay, reader, look:
at some level you already know everything
written in the present tense is a lie. This is not
an exception. Fourth wall or no, there's a third person
here, the second I,
the realer one, disingenuously
obscuring herself while simultaneously
recreating the other. The two of us,

she and I, past and present: now we're assembling
together on the page
a story that she alone could not have told
then as it unfolded faster
than conscious thought, faster
than the starlight that came to shine and burn and die

on the time and place where she was I. Soon
he'll be trapped

like she was then, desperately
willing the night to end, stuck in
the viscous thick of muteness as her friend
who insisted he didn't like her
like that, denied and denied wanting
to fuck her (*though we might
refer to that as making love*, he once wrote
in a reply to one of her messages, objecting to her blunt force
verb choice), unfurled his romantic calendar for the week.
But no. Nobody calls it that.
Probably needless to say, I've always found ruin

more satisfying than creation. The best
part of writing poetry is breaking
the lines, kicking a foot out and tripping
the syntax, exposing the raw nerves,
the awkward ambiguities, the bloody beating
heart of things. Hitting the page, coming apart
and together with a violence at once
predictable and singular, like a body
landing. A splattery mess. *A brain crush*

is what he named his feelings for me.
Yes. That. He was an artist too,
a painter. "I could paint you," he'd say,
and it visibly scared the shit out of me,
and he loved that. He loved seeing

any type of reaction on my face. I see now
how these simple facts read just as well as metaphors
for the intimacy between us
and for the lack of it. I wonder sometimes if he ever did
paint me, or even wanted to. Possibly the threat's real
purpose was just to show me how I looked
to him: unwilling, hostile
muse raging against her own physicality.
Strange, frustrating woman offering
nothing to him, nothing but language and silence.
I did not want
to be painted. *I don't need your permission*,
he pointed out. True. If you ask me,
artistic licence is absolute.
So here we are. There he is

asking her something about the holidays
just past, trying
to make conversation, trying so hard to draw her
back to herself, to him, but I've already told you
it's too late. "Is this conversation hard for you?"
he asks. This situation is hard for me,
she thinks, her mind travelling further
and further away. We are near
crying, she and I, unravelling, there and here,
then and now. This poem is hard for me.
But hey, look, at last, we're reaching
the end. It's over.

—from PRISM *international*

Sadie McCarney

SELF-PORTRAIT AS DIANA, VIRGIN
GODDESS OF THE MOON AND THE HUNT

So now I'm the moon: pallid
and huge, with so many phases
of wanting and then not wanting
a body. Your body. I crave the kind

of kiss where The Other has pitched
a tent in my tonsils. I study kisses.
Then, I do fieldwork and find results
that do not match my thought-out

hypotheses: tongue sandpapery,
rough like a cat's. Or lip-glossed
mouth locked up, like the front
of a foreclosed house. I think

I want the penne I ordered, then
as it comes piping tableside
I develop, suddenly, an allergy
to wheat. I give out dating tips

like Hallowe'en sweets, but each
time I get a Plenty Of Fish missive
I shut my browser and moan. I want—
what? A rom-com life? I once had

a date where we did Wholesome
Date Things, like checking off a list:
dinner, chitchat, ice cream, a long
walk, even snogging in the park.

But you can't make a puzzle fit
grass into pieces of sky. I have
wanted ~~a girlfriend~~ the idea of a girlfriend
since Grade Three, when with sweat-

sodden palms I asked the pretty,
blonde New Girl in Class to be
my very best friend. But I have paid
for numerous solutions: speed dating/

with algorithms/ for asexuals/ for queers/
for us, the increasingly desperate few.
I wanted it all, until I didn't want it at all.
I am predictable as the Moon's wax

and wane. It's like with gallery nudes:
you can admire the curvature of
Venus' ass without taking her out
to drink moonshine and dance.

—from *Grain*

Nancy Jo Cullen

SPACE

But maybe this is all mood is, rising grief and its ebb then a winter chickadee on the sand cherry tree. I can write about my dog leaping over a puddle (darling! darling!) but not about my children. Such a terrible affection. They lived in my body and then they didn't. They rubbed my earlobes and then they didn't. It is entire or it is abject. I am weary of not being young anymore.

And so my dog jumps over the puddle like a tiny gazelle, like a white-tailed deer bounding across a paved road in the back-country, except she is neither antelope nor cervine. Later the dog will take her place at the foot of my bed and I might think again about my children pressed against me in sleep when all I wanted was a little freedom, a little space of my own.

—from *The Ex-Puritan*

Monty Reid

SPRING RIDER

The teeter-totter won't lift my feet
off the ground.

The spring-mounted hippo keels over forward
when I get on.
               No bounce.

The playground sand, trucked in from somewhere
that has worn it smooth
                    gets in my nose.

Everything is too small.

The sneaker—left foot

the plastic bucket

the stars.

—from *filling Station*

Erin Conway-Smith

STILL, NIGHT THOUGHTS

A fresh metre between fact and feeling.
I've strapped on the snowshoes so
I'll only sink mid-Sorel.

The greyscale, the hush ... I'd forgotten
this photocopied landscape for a long while
but it's back with a pang I fought to leave.

My father sends photos of pine grosbeaks
feeding. Security cam captures of a wolf
at the door. Winter disappears the house

or makes it. What would I even do there.
How would I square it
with my grasping younger self

which is also my old self, although
my way of speaking betrays me.
A light dusting of existential questions

I won't exactly contemplate.
There's the truck stop
and then there's the turn off:

I still drive it in my dreams.
And the people in that place,
which used to be me

they brush their cars in the mornings
so they can see.

They're seeing the road.
They're going slow.

—from PRISM *international*

Nina Berkhout

A STUDY IN COATS

I enjoyed the program, my aging
father tells me, but these TV actors
all put their coats on in the same
ridiculous way. They must learn
from one book. You didn't notice?

I didn't.

Well, they swing their coat
like a cape and it goes flying around
over the shoulder. Were it you or me
we would break things.
We'd never get our arms in.

He waits on the phone. I hear him breathing.

I try to recall scenes of coats
worn with humility, picturing instead
my father leaving for work in the dark
each morning, a calligraphy of threads
hanging from his jacket lining.

I want to say, suspension of disbelief.
But maybe there comes a point
where you need to see

the struggle. The stiff movements
and the fight with zip and buttons.

And did you ever notice, I finally ask back,
how someone being chased
runs straight ahead till what's behind
mows them down, when all
they had to do was step aside?

Of course, he replies.
They stole that from our dreams.

—from *Canadian Literature*

Rob Taylor

SUNLIGHT

I no longer remember
the blessed black object
my daughter dropped
in deep snow

only the mile out
and the mile back
in the deep pines
alone.

—from the *Literary Review of Canada*

Jean Eng

TAI CHI IN THE SNOW

Stars dissolve moments
after they land on my shoulder.

Blue spruce and white pine
shrug: yet another dwarf

planet and its repository of
quiet collisions. Variations

on a pentagram, diatom or
mandala open the space

between words my body
moves through and out of

the way. A new species of
religion discovered every day.

—from *The Fiddlehead*

Rhiannon Ng Cheng Hin

TELEPHONE REPAIRMAN

I found a hammer on the Cat's Back,
lodged in tall grass, tektite-strewn dirt
oxidizing its claw in summit haze.
There's a thought, evidence of the
intractable—a figure in faded linen
drifting from pole
to pole, tool box in hand.
I could become a telephone repairman,
rest between jobs by bell ponds
and calving brume, exist only
as interstitial noise.
I could take this hammer and drive it
through a wet-oak memory of itself
or find its owner's grave and return it
to his earthen fist. I could use this
hammer to hale clouds from ragged
frames, pull them down, down across
bleak signal lights, down beneath
these insufferable wires, down
into unanswerable peat.

—from *The Walrus*

Francesca Schulz-Bianco

10 EASY STEPS TO MY BODY

Before I was born,
my body was the whole event,
an upbeat, rhyming picture book.

My parents stayed home all night
downloading my body, my body.

I saw my body coming out of the water, a bronzed,
turquoise bust. A little boy on the beach pointed
and started to cry.

Is this my body?
That thing the sky has pinned to the ground?

In the Valley of the Temples
my body is a green walnut, its sandpaper
shell stains my body violet-black.

Dry grass, my body is the dry
grass between broken columns, waving.

Body, where have you gone?

Didn't you know you are the ultimate gift
for future generations?

"The eye is the lamp of the body"
so says the Sermon on the Mount.
Forgive me, I did not know:

I'm not always
where my body is.

—from *The Malahat Review*

T. Liem

THERE ARE NO ACTUAL MONSTERS
IN THIS POEM I HOPE

Stitches in her chin, bikes abandoned at the bottom of a hill,
an orange sky.

Decades pass and I'm still oozing down looking at her
saying I love you.

I didn't say it then, but I say it now.
Also known as being fashionably late.

Walking up, we cupped our hands under her chin, taking care
to save the street from being stained.

Also known as protecting what hurt us.

Moments earlier we were thrilled by the laws of gravity
pulling us on our bikes and she coasted until a pothole threw her.

To say what it meant would be deceptive, but I've done it,
citing the time we kissed as the first sign

of something that might burst open
if never spoken. And I'll do it again.

At the time we didn't have the words to chew through.
Like a mouth, language can be bite, lick, and kiss.

We were smooth, young, pretty. We sat under a desk.
We were girls

playing a game we called party.
It was day and we were alone.

Decades pass and I wake with a sandpaper tongue
wondering if it was just me

under the desk
drooling.

Have you ever picked at your past until it's all drip and shine?
Just me?

I've been keeping a list of the ways I am monstrous
and let me tell you how it ends:

On a hill. Mouth full, slow, open.

—from *The Malahat Review*

Kayla Czaga

THIRTEEN YEARS

I never believed the story you told me about the girl
who came into the bookstore you worked at
and then drowned herself in the ocean a few days later.

You'd avoided her pretty, desperate face in the aisles,
had jokingly recommended Mrs. Dalloway
when she cornered you for books about suicide.

The girl, Virginia Woolf, stones in both their pockets—
it fit too well together. I assumed you were trying
to tell me about yourself but had to use the girl to do it.

That fall, you wrote a poem about the tide bearing her body
away like a bottle with a note curled up inside it.
Our writing group loved that poem. I did too,

even if I didn't believe it. I wrote tiny poems,
stripped to nouns and verbs, a kind of writing
someone might admire but never love.

We drank wine on beaches, then waded in.
When water weighed down our tights, we tied them
around our necks, sliced our bare feet on stones.

Years later, I asked what had happened
to that poem and you told me you'd tried editing it,
but every line was bad. Every line? I doubted that

the way I doubted the story itself and the others
you've told before and since, brimming with coincidence,
characters resurfacing as if in a novel.

We live in separate cities now. Hundreds of people
like the filtered images you share of your life
while I post fewer and fewer photos. We've been friends

for thirteen years and I don't know how many times
you've wanted to die. I want you to tell me this fact,
awful as a body hauled in on the tide. Tell me the story

you started years ago, about being cornered by yourself
and laughing your way out of it. Maybe it's me
who needs passing encounters to mean something,

who can't just let stories squawk from far-off rocks.
For thirteen years you've told me I'm too honest
and I know you're right. I walk to the beach

to watch the ocean's great grey breathing and wonder
which stones you would choose, knowing
they'd be indistinguishable from mine.

—from The New Quarterly

Barbara Nickel

THREE-IN-ONE

1. Eve weeds the winter garden

from hardpan soil
pulls roots, hairy hosts—
bindweed,
quack grass,
thistle—
iron for the compost
she'll dig in around the ghost bramble's
silver canes, now
you see them
now
you don't
in early morning light, pawprints
over frost, in her ear the voices long
and freshly gone.

Eve pulls oxalis from the dead
woolly thyme, finds
pleasure in cutting
back, running
her fingertip along a bristled stalk
young from coppicing
while its fruit, edible
but unexceptional, is seldom seen.

Loss divides to multiply.
Canes spring
in a sheen
of midwinter sun.

2. Maeshowe

Midwinter sun along
the passage grave we crouch to enter—
mound on a turf disc within a ditch ringed
by a wall. Seen from above, a kind of dartboard;
we are crawling to the bull's eye.
Please don't touch the walls. Made of stone, cut
and carried without metal tools. Precise light.
In the central chamber, up high,
see where the Norse broke in
and carved graffiti runes: Benedikt made this cross. Trying
to not touch, and to listen hard, I,
this—we are all eclipsed by a rustle, a swallow sudden
in our talk and remember
she was feeding her young in the inmost chamber.

3. The Running Potter and the Wind

In the inmost chamber unthinkable is the boy with his class on
the river trail a few blocks from here, preschoolers in file, each
with a backpack containing a snack and a water bottle. Fine
day, no wind, a teacher at the front, at the back, and in between
a falling tree. I try not to dwell here, avoid telling the story but
late one night read the teacher's tribute. She'd taught my own.

It was the beavers' fault for whittling the trunk to its tipping point and the trail committee will ensure this won't happen again.

November on a walk, I meet a potter friend out for a run and she mentions the parents have asked her to make their son's urn. I think the wind rose between us just as she was saying *keep forming as it's formed* and I'm walking this place beside the stalwart quaking trees, seeing a friend squatting on the creek bed, digging up muck and clay, shaping a ball from hard-pan soil.

—from *Grain*

John Steffler

UNWELCOME SCENE

There's no use telling yourself be careful
what you dread. A world soundless, voiceless.
Flailing in dark ocean swell. Your house
and surrounding trees burnt. The studio
that churns out those scenes has no address.
You can't call to be taken off their list.
In a dream a parade is passing—shrill
bands on wagons, sequinned emperors, stilts—
no one will look at you alone on the sidewalk.
You wake up in tears. And then the person
you've shared a life with really leaves you,
and there you are on a corner watching
your life-mate cross on the far side—arm
in arm with someone you've never seen—such
buoyant grace—sunlight—a breeze playing
in their hair. It will come. What haunts you
most. You attract it. Why do I feel it's
the poet's job to say this? What creeps
in from the moment's edges, wrecking it, is
the knowledge of what you'll face. What
can you do but try to make friends with it—
or art?

—from *Arc Poetry Magazine*

Lisa Richter

WHATEVER IT TAKES

What a fluke: spring's love language
is endless drizzle, mine the need to complain
about it. A white moth, alleged spirit of a lost
loved one returning to this world for a brief hang,
flickers past me in my parking-lot-turned-garden,
where I lounge in a grungy white plastic chair
like I'm poolside in Cabo. What would my father
think about taking on such a dainty appearance—
pale wings like cherry blossoms—a man who once
rejected a reusable grocery bag with a flower on it,
asking if I had anything "less feminine."
These days, I thirst for anything the least bit
fabulous. Last night in the ER, where I awaited
answers on a racing heart, a woman in a wheelchair,
bald but for a dusting of fine silver fuzz, rocked
a sensational pair of knee-high black leather boots.
I wanted to compliment her on them but thought
it best to stay within my Plexiglass partition.
A security guard came up and gently draped
a blue-and-white blanket around her shoulders,
which she drew over her head like a rabbi in a tallit.
As I write this, a seedpod from the tree
above me spirals into my lap. My Portuguese
neighbours are grilling sardines again,
transporting me to the Azores. If I were clean

laundry hanging on the line, by now
I'd be close to dry, smelling faintly of rain
and fresh thyme, with maybe a touch of smoke.

—from The Fiddlehead

CONTRIBUTORS' COMMENTARY AND BIOGRAPHIES

DAVID BARRICK lives in London, Ontario (London Township Treaty 6). He is the author of the poetry collection *Nightlight* (Palimpsest, 2022) as well as two chapbooks. His poems appear in *Grain*, *The Fiddlehead*, *Arc Poetry Magazine*, *The Malahat Review*, *subTerrain*, *Prairie Fire*, and other literary journals. He teaches writing at Western University and is the managing director of Antler River Poetry.

Barrick writes, "Bob Ross didn't always have an easy life, but there's something almost mythically serene about his televised persona. At the height of the pandemic, my wife and I went through a phase of watching episode after episode of *The Joy of Painting*. I wrote 'Bob Ross Beats the Devil' in April 2022, around the time that our cat Tobi needed some teeth removed and the cumulative stress of the past two years was taking its toll. The poem seemed to capture the tentative optimism of moving through that moment."

NINA BERKHOUT lives in Ottawa and is the author of several poetry collections and novels, most recently *Why Birds Sing*

(ECW Press, 2020), which was named a "must-read" by the *Globe and Mail.*

Berkhout writes, "I have lived on the other side of the country from my parents for many years. 'A Study in Coats' came about during one of our weekly phone calls. Sometimes I grow impatient at their stories. Only after hanging up do I think, wait. There is something to this. The dialogue in the first half of the poem actually happened. The second half is me continuing our talk alone, after we said goodbye. Stretching the tale to reach a truth, as we do in poetry. Growing up, my dad was all about routine, hard work, devotion. Attributes that served him well as a geriatrician, and which guide me in the writing life. Someday, I'll probably write about his morning porridge. Or my mother's drawerfuls of pencils worn to the nub from grading, sketching, grocery lists. If I listen, I'll find a poem in nearly every conversation I have had with my parents, their observations far more insightful than mine. And, one day, I suppose, a poem will arise from the absence of those conversations. The missed calls."

NICHOLAS BRADLEY lives in Victoria, British Columbia—in ləkʷəŋən territory. He is the author of two books of poetry: *Rain Shadow* (University of Alberta Press, 2018) and *Before Combustion* (Gaspereau Press, 2023). He teaches in the Department of English at the University of Victoria.

Of "Atmospheric River," Bradley writes, "In the late autumn of 2021, British Columbia and the state of Washington suffered calamitous flooding as a result of extraordinary rain. The so-called atmospheric river—the term was suddenly on everyone's lips—led to what has been deemed the costliest natural disaster in the history of the province. An old friend in Calgary told me that the phrase was new to him, which gave me an opening. In the rest of the poem, I tried to suggest the difficulty of finding the right words for an almost unimaginable event. But I also hoped to show that during a crisis—now our permanent condition, it seems—language, art, and friendship persist. We go on, and a poem might cross the mountains even when the highways are closed. I can't think of rivers in the Pacific Northwest without thinking of Richard Hugo, and I borrowed a thing or two from his poetry. He died before I might have met him, but I like to imagine that our poems give each other a cordial nod."

ALISON BRAID is a writer from the Okanagan. She is the author of the chapbook *Little Hunches* (Anstruther Press, 2020). Her prose and poetry have appeared in magazines such as *West Branch*, *The Adroit Journal*, PRISM international, *The New Quarterly*, *Grain*, and *Arc Poetry Magazine*.

Of "Fear of Desire," Braid writes, "For three years, I lived in Prague, teaching English. The first year, I worked at a kindergarten where we sang, put on plays, and made crafts. We used flashcards, taught words like *snow*, *swim*, *duck*. For me, it was a brand-new entry point into the English language. I was, at the same time, falling in love with my teaching partner. We would leave school together and walk to the tram stop, and one day, came upon the carp in the underpass. All this to say: there was a lot of newness in my life—the newness of seeing language as a newcomer sees it, the newness of new love, the newness of the new customs that surrounded me. I think perhaps I am most attentive to a place when I'm missing it, and so I didn't write the poem until much later, when I had some distance and was living in Vancouver. As I wrote, those two images kept surfacing in my mind: Julia and the frost, and the carp in their buckets. I didn't know what those two images had in common. I had to put them on the page to find out."

LOUISE CARSON studied music in Montreal and Toronto, played jazz piano and sang in the chorus of the Canadian Opera Company. She's published fourteen books, including two collections of poetry: *Dog Poems* (Aeolus House) in 2020 and *A Clearing* (Signature Editions) in 2015. She also writes mysteries and historical fiction. Her two latest books are *The Last Unsuitable Man* (Signature Editions, 2022) and *Third Circle* (land/sea press, 2022). When not writing, she shovels snow, runs, or gardens.

Carson writes, "When I'm writing poetry, which I tend to do in batches, I give units of poems names: Different; New Stages; Next Level; Use Everything. When I wrote 'Little fires,' I'd just finished a hefty bunch of poems called 'Rewire the Brain,' in the writing of which, said brain started to get a bit fevered. I think I was trying too hard. So, 'Little fires' was the first poem I wrote after I closed Rewire and took a deep breath, stepping back. It gave the next unit its name. (And dibble is one of my favourite words, ever.)"

HILARY CLARK lives in Victoria, British Columbia. She is retired from teaching English at U of Saskatchewan for many years. She is the author of *The Dwelling of Weather* and *More Light*, both from Brick Books, and *Two Heavens* from Hagios. *More Light* won the Pat Lowther Award and the Anne Szumigalski Award (SK) in 1999. Clark translates French surrealist poetry and has published both her own poems and her translations in overseas surrealist magazines.

Clark writes, "The prose poems here are taken from a sequence of 124 dated poems titled 'My Muted Year.' These run from the last part of 2019, before the world became aware of COVID, through 2020, the year of the plague and lockdowns: four seasons of world crisis. But the sequence is not *about* COVID; it is not about any single theme or unifying metaphor. The poems touch on other crisis topics such as urban homelessness and climate disaster; in fact, they pull in everything but the kitchen sink in fragments arranged not by narrative or logical coherence but by repetition and the associative logic of dreams. Multiple fragments, multiple voices: 'My Muted Year' is the journal of a subject (one step aside from the author), an aging poet whose lyric expressions are ridiculed or attacked by other voices."

ERIN CONWAY-SMITH lives in Johannesburg, South Africa. She was born and raised in Thunder Bay, Ontario. Her journalism has appeared in the *Economist*, the *Times*, *Foreign Policy*, the *Globe and Mail*, and many other places. Her poems have been published by *The Malahat Review*, PRISM *international*, and *Ons Klyntji*. Erin won the University of Toronto's 2019 Janice Colbert Poetry Award.

Conway-Smith writes, "I wasn't able to return to Canada for a few years. During a bout of homesickness, I found myself thinking about winter things that were once ordinary but had become foreign to me (it really had been a long while). I was also re-reading Tang dynasty poetry—I lived in Beijing before moving to Johannesburg—and I had Li Bai's famous 'Jing Ye Si' in my ears, a poem heavy with longing for home. But missing home can be complicated. As a teenager, like many people from remote towns, I was desperate to leave Thunder Bay. I wanted to get as far away as possible. Now, after many years away, flying over the Sleeping Giant and into the city is one of my favourite views in the world."

NANCY JO CULLEN lives in Kingston, Ontario. Her fourth poetry collection, published by Wolsak and Wynn, is *Nothing Will Save Your Life*. Her poetry and fiction have appeared in *The Puritan*, *Grain*, *filling Station*, *Plenitude Magazine*, *Prairie Fire*, *Arc Poetry Magazine*, *This Magazine*, *Best Canadian Poetry 2018*, *Room*, *The Journey Prize*, and *Best Canadian Fiction 2012*. Nancy is the 2010 recipient of the Dayne Ogilvie Prize for LGBTQ+ Emerging Writers. Her novel, *The Western Alienation Merit Badge* (Wolsak and Wynn, 2019), was shortlisted for the 2020 Amazon Canada First Novel Award.

Cullen writes, "In writing 'Space' I was thinking about all those years of parenting when I longed for this moment in time when, finally, I would have some distance from my children and all their needs and mess and drama. So, of course, it was an awful surprise to discover I would feel such grief after my children and I launched into our separate lives. It's always felt difficult to write about my kids, to express anything meaningful about how complicated and big my love for them is without being terribly cliché. This poem is trying to grapple with this problem."

KAYLA CZAGA lives in Victoria, British Columbia. She is the author of *For Your Safety Please Hold On* (Nightwood Editions, 2014), which won the Gerald Lampert Memorial Award and was shortlisted for the Governor General's Award for Poetry, and *Dunk Tank* (House of Anansi Press, 2019), which was nominated for the Dorothy Livesay Poetry Prize. Her third collection, *Midway*, is forthcoming from House of Anansi in 2023.

Czaga writes, "I began writing 'Thirteen Years' a couple of months after I moved back to Victoria in 2019. I lived right across the street from the beach, and frequently staring at the ocean made me remember the story of the poem—the story of a girl who may or may not have drowned. It took a long time for me to get this poem right. At first, it was shorter and much shallower. I made it about a lot of different things before I realized what I essentially wanted to talk about was storytelling. My speaker was frustrated that she felt her friend's storytelling was less truthful than her own, and she believed that their diverging narratives created a barrier between the two of them; she felt as if she couldn't connect with her friend because she didn't know if she was ever being told the truth, being let in on how her friend was actually feeling. Once I figured that was what I wanted to say, the poem stretched out its legs and began to walk around in itself, but it came with the realization that there is no 'honest' storytelling, that all stories have a particular lens, which warps and colours the so-called facts. The slow process of writing this poem (of retelling the story) is almost proof of that. The connection my speaker craved came in this realization that both her and her friend were flawed storytellers. And, suddenly, they could be flawed together."

ROCCO DE GIACOMO lives in Toronto with his wife, Lisa Keophila, a fabric artist, and his daughters, Ava and Matilda. He is a widely published poet whose work has appeared in literary journals in Canada, Australia, England, Hong Kong, and the US. The author of numerous poetry chapbooks and full-length collections, his latest, *Casting Out* (Guernica Editions)—on the reconciliation of the author's secular lifestyle and their deeply Evangelical upbringing—was published in April of 2023.

Of "Not Until It Does," de Giacomo writes, "It is part of a larger project entitled *Slow Wrestle the Moon*. This project is an attempt to create a clearer, more distilled picture of the human animal by focusing on the connections between human biology and the cosmos. Through these connections, it is my intention to remind the reader that all ideas and emotions are physical processes intrinsically part of a vast physical universe. As science writer Michael Brooks points out, 'Every advance [in science] will most likely tell us as much about ourselves as it will about the universe we inhabit. We are all collections of chemicals made in the cataclysmic explosions of stars; we are stardust, or nuclear waste . . .' I am approaching these poems from the perspective that everything we are, everything we know, comes from a star."

JEAN ENG is a visual artist and poet from Toronto. She is the author of *Festival of All Souls* (Inanna Publications, 2020) a debut collection of poetry. Her writing has appeared in journals from Canada, the US, and the United Kingdom. These include *Contemporary Verse 2*, *Fiddlehead*, *Grain*, *The New Quarterly*, *Room*, and *Vallum*. She has work forthcoming in *Queen's Quarterly*.

Eng writes, "The slow, contemplative movements of tai chi, executed by groups or individuals in an outdoor setting, usually occur during warm weather seasons. For 'Tai Chi in the Snow' I wanted to capture the experience of doing Classical Yang Family–style tai chi in my neighbourhood park, solo on a winter's day. In addition to colder temperatures, the challenge of doing tai chi outside involved specific movements performed while bulked up with extra clothing: coat, boots, hat, gloves. There were safety concerns, too, like wind, visibility, potentially slippery surfaces: parts of the set include balancing on one leg, kicks, stepping backwards. A mild afternoon helped. Although clumsier and less adept, I discovered that the additional weight of garments, greater vigilance and caution, actually slowed me down to the point where I became more present with both the moves and my surroundings than any tai chi recently practised indoors."

JOEL ROBERT FERGUSON grew up in the village of Bible Hill (seriously), Nova Scotia, and now lives in Winnipeg, where he is a PhD candidate at the University of Manitoba. He is the author of *The Lost Cafeteria* (Signature Editions, 2020) (winner of the Lansdowne Prize for Poetry). His writing has appeared in *Arc Poetry Magazine*, *The Malahat Review*, *Prairie Fire*, *Qwerty*, and elsewhere.

Ferguson writes, "I composed these sections of my ongoing long poem 'Last Things Lasting' in the fall of 2021; they are derived from notes taken while driving from Winnipeg to Nova Scotia and back with my partner and their brother during the second summer of the pandemic. At the time of our trip, a goodly portion of Northern Ontario seemed to be on fire or smoke-saturated, and the news on the radio was focused primarily on the collapse of the West's imperial misadventure in Afghanistan, so the language and overall tone of the poem is that of the every-day-apocalyptic/banal-dystopic that was (is) literally in the air. I opted for the use of (mostly) long lines because I both enjoy playing fragments and truncated sentences within their loosened restraints, and as an attempt to convey a feeling of inexorable horizon(tal)-vectored movement."

SUSAN GILLIS has lived on the east and west coasts of Canada and now makes her home in rural Ontario, on traditional Omàmìwininì (Algonquin) territory. She has published four books of poetry, most recently *Yellow Crane* (Brick, 2018), and is a member of the collaborative group Yoko's Dogs.

Of "Moving Day," Gillis writes: "The day my father moved into long-term care, he asked me to tour him around the building so he could take the measure of his new home, inside and out. This poem maps that exploration. I'm interested in how stored emotion can flare up unexpectedly out of random clusters of colour, light, and form. Here, a clump of dry field grass sparks the memory of torn-up baseboard, and re-ignites the turbulence of that day."

Trans writer LUKE HATHAWAY lives in Kjipuktuk/Halifax and teaches at Saint Mary's University. His book *The Affirmations* (Biblioasis, 2022) was named a best book of the year by the *Times* (London, UK) in 2022. He often writes words for music and—a performer as well as a poet—he is enamoured of the stage. He frequently collaborates with singer/scholar Daniel Cabena as part of the metamorphosing ensemble ANIMA.

Of "Ballad," Hathaway writes, "I had the good fortune to grow up surrounded by storytellers. I heard the Irish selkie stories for the first time when I was still a child, and they have stayed with me. They were part of the mythological language of transness that I inherited from my people—from my various peoples—long before I had languages that could operate in the social, legal, and/or medical spheres. Those other languages have not replaced the mythopoeic, for me; they have affirmed it. At the same time, they need to return to the mythopoeic to replenish themselves from time to time: transitions are almost always more complicated than we give them credit for. There are the social, legal, and medical stories, but there is also a spiritual story; there are gender transitions, but there are also transitions that take us across the boundary between life and death, between one existence and another, across the lines between species ... My poem tells a spiritual story of transition, using a language I had with me at the time of the writing. It was set to music by my dear friend the singer/scholar Daniel Cabena, in whose piercing countertenor one can hear the song performed on the website of *The Walrus* magazine, where the poem was first published (thewalrus.ca/ballad). Some of the lines in the poem have their origin in oral material collected and translated by David Thomson in his book *The People of the Sea* (Turnstile Press, 1954)."

BEATRIZ HAUSNER is a Toronto poet, and the author of several poetry collections, including *Beloved Revolutionary Sweetheart* (Book*hug Press, 2020), and *She Who Lies Above* (Book*hug Press, 2023). Her books have been published internationally in translation, including her native Spanish. Hausner's work as a literary historian and translator of surrealism has exerted an important influence on her own writing. Hausner is a respected editor and critic, was a founding publisher of Quattro Books, and was Chair of the Public Lending Right Commission.

Hausner writes, "'The Orgasms Room,' forms part of *Secrets of the House on Rue du Château*, a work whose naissance dates back to the 'The Reverse of the Gaze,' a surrealist exhibition and festival I participated in in Coimbra, Portugal, in May 2008. At the time, I was in the process of writing *Enter the Raccoon* (Book*hug Press, 2012), a book of prose poetics, which my surrealist friends found befitting of the occasion. It was Miguel de Carvalho, the organizer and host of that large international gathering, who suggested I collaborate with the Dutch surrealist artist Rik Lina and create parallel writings to a series of ink-on-paper drawings Rik titled 'The Secret Life of Plants.' Very naturally, I applied a technique I favour, where I riff off others' art and allow the associative process to do the rest. A narrative voice in me quickly emerged, guiding me as I wove textual images and sounds into the memory of a book I had read when I was in my twenties, André Thirion's memoir *Revolutionaries Without Revolution* (MacMillan, 1975). In it, Thirion relates how during a short period, from about 1926–1932, he lived in a house on Rue du Château in Paris. What stayed with me was the fact of the freedom with which surrealist artists and writers lived there, sometimes briefly, other times less so, always creatively and innovatively."

ROBERT HOGG (1942–2022) was a retired English professor and organic farmer who wrote from his farm in Eastern Ontario. He published five books of poetry, and six chapbooks; his work has appeared in periodicals, including *Pamenar Online*, *The Café Review*, *Dispatches*, *Arc Poetry Magazine*, *The Typescript*, *Ottawater 16*, and *Periodicities*, among others. Recent chapbooks include: *from LAMENTATIONS* (above/ground), *Ranch Days— for Ed Dorn* (Battleaxe), *Ranch Days—the McIntosh* (Hawk/ weed) *A Quiet Affair—Vanc '63* (Trainwreck), *The Red Menace* (Hogwallow) and *Apothegms* (Apt 9). His forthcoming books include *Postcards, from and to America* from CHAX Press, and *Not to Call it Chaos—The Vancouver Poems* from Ekstasis.

EVAN JONES (Ευριπίδης Ιωάννου) was born in Weston, Ontario, and has lived in Manchester, UK, since 2005. His most recent book of poems is *Later Emperors* (Carcanet, 2020). *The Barbarians Arrive Today: Poems and Prose of C.P. Cavafy* (Carcanet, 2020) was a TLS Book of the Year.

CONSTANTINE PETROU CAVAFY (1863–1933) was born in Alexandria, Egypt, where, for thirty years, he was employed at the Irrigation Office of the Ministry of Public Works (Third Circle). As a child, he lived and was educated in London and Liverpool.

Jones writes, "The English that I have translated the Alexandrian Greek poet Cavafy (1863–1933) into is not my own. I researched and read many of his sources and inspirations—Gibbon, Baudelaire, Plutarch, Anna Komnene. My aim was to understand where his poems came from: Enlightenment history somehow meets French *fin de siècle* decadence, ancient morality and Modernism in 'He planned to read.' It is magical and frustrating to approach as a translator. Cavafy's syntax is usually straightforward, and sentences rarely extend further than two or three lines. Adjectives are sparse and simple. He was born in Alexandria to Constantinopolitan Greek parents, immigrants, and went to school as a young boy in Liverpool and London, where his father's company had offices. There is a joke, a rumour, that the British-educated Cavafy spoke Greek with an English lilt. In some ways his syntax and language reflect this. But there is a misconception that his poems are prosaic. They are, in the sense that they do not meander or prettify. But they are never wordy or verbose and sound is always key. Modern Greek is full of diphthongs, for instance, Cavafy's control of vowels is telling. If the poem reminds you a bit of this century and a bit of centuries long past us, that is about right."

MEGHAN KEMP-GEE lives between North Vancouver and Fredericton, where she is a PhD candidate at UNB. She is the author of two chapbooks and *The Animal in the Room* (Coach House, 2023). She also co-created *Contested Strip*, the world's best comic about ultimate frisbee (and soon to be a graphic novel).

Of "A Newly Discovered Species of Lizard with Distinctive Triangular Scales," Kemp-Gee writes, "Most of the details in this poem are entirely made up ... But Darwin really did eat owl flesh at Cambridge University! He was the founder of the Glutton Club, where they dined on unusual 'birds and beasts.' This lizard comes from a longer series of animal poems in which I play with evolutionary biology as a metaphor for lyric forms and mental illness. I think the speaker is a version of me as an overly enthusiastic nineteenth-century naturalist. This character loves the idea of newness and discovery, but he finds that there are alien creatures all around him, full of troubling genetic codes and dangerous patterns. Nothing he 'discovers' is as new as he imagined. We're always getting in over our heads."

JOSEPH KIDNEY is originally from New Westminster, British Columbia. He won the Short Grain Contest from *Grain* and The Young Buck Poetry Prize (now The Foster Prize) from CV2. His chapbook, *Terra Firma, Pharma Sea* is available from Anstruther Press. He is completing a PhD on Renaissance English drama at Stanford University.

Of "Oscail Do Bhéal," Kidney writes, "Sometimes when I have walked through art galleries, I have envied the artistic situation of painters who decided, or perhaps rather were compelled by some kind of scarcity, to paint portraits of family members. When I began writing this (COVID era) poem, which took about a month to complete, I had been feeling low about pretty much everything, and poetry in particular seemed like an activity so grotesquely self-interested that a moral person would stop at nothing to avoid being so incriminated. Something resembling family portraits, however, might amount, I thought, to a loophole. Material testaments of gratitude. That sort of thing. The idea is not without its flaws. This kind of domestic poem can often be a kind of narcissism disguised as outward-facing tenderness. Surely, I have sketched myself here too. And I can hear Jimmy Stewart at the end of *Vertigo*: you shudna been that senna-mennal. The exact and exaggerated intonation of 'I'll say a Hail Mary / for you' comes from an audiobook recording of the end of James Joyce's 'Counterparts.' Fans of the Bible and/or funerals will recognize borrowings from 1 Corinthians 15 and Psalm 90 in the third section. If you ever come across me taking out the recycling, listen closely and you will hear, barely audible, the muttered liturgy of resurrection from the office for the burial of the dead."

MATTHEW KING lives in what Al Purdy called "the country north of Belleville," where he tries to grow things, counts birds, and takes pictures of flowers with bugs on them. He was the winner of the 2020/2021 *FreeFall Magazine* poetry contest and has published poems in places including *The New Quarterly* and *Rattle*. Previously, he taught philosophy at York University, and published a book called *Heidegger and Happiness* (Bloomsbury Academic, 2009).

King writes, "I wrote the first three stanzas of 'On the Ducks Who Are People and the Ducks Who Are Ducks,' surprisingly exactly as they appear here, on National Drunk Writing Night, 2020 (a bottle of red wine and some whisky in). NaDruWriNi—an occasion someone came up with long ago to lubricate the creative engines of National Novel Writing Month (NaNoWriMo) participants, kept alive in recent years as a kind of high feast by a few weirdos such as myself—is the first Saturday in November, which is in the middle of duck-hunting season. Duck-hunting season upsets me a lot. That upset and its grounds are pretty plain in the poem. All perceiving beings, ducks as much as us, are, I think, sites where being lights up. The difference between non-human animals, such as ducks, and us is that we can know this and respond to the lighting-up of being as the unfathomable wonder it is. But mostly it seems we don't know it. Mostly we ignore it, if not outright deny it, for instance by mixing it up with the strictly physical cause-and-effect processes of AIs, and so we are alienated from the most important thing about ourselves. A lot of my poems have to do with how seeing the ways in which we are like and unlike non-human animals allows us to understand ourselves better; this poem has to do with the most fundamental of those ways."

SARAH LACHMANSINGH is a Guyanese-Canadian writer from Toronto. She studied writing at the University of Victoria, and is a fiction intern at *The Malahat Review*. In 2021, she was selected as a mentee for BIPOC Writers Connect. Her work has appeared in *Homology Lit*, *filling Station*, *Augur Magazine*, EVENT, *The / tƐmz/ Review*, and elsewhere. She is working on a novel.

Lachmansingh writes, "I wanted to capture a sense of dream-like dread in 'he hasn't arrived and someone has turned on the streetlamps.' When drafting this poem, I remember thinking about that moment when streetlamps seem to suddenly flick on, and how uncanny the shift into night can sometimes feel. I knew I wanted this idea of arrival to remain open-ended, as there's a liminal undercurrent of anticipation brewing in the poem's atmosphere."

T. LIEM lives in Montreal, aka Tio'Tia:ke, unceded Kan-ien'kehá:ka territories. They are the author of *Slows: Twice* (Coach House, 2023), and *Obits.* (Coach House, 2018), which was shortlisted for a Lambda Literary Award, and won the Ger-ald Lampert Memorial Award as well as the A.M. Klein Prize. Their writing has been published in *Apogee, Plenitude Maga-zine, The Boston Review, Grain, Maisonneuve, Catapult, The Malahat Review, The Fiddlehead*, and elsewhere.

Of "There Are No Actual Monsters in This Poem I Hope," Liem writes, "I heard K-Ming Chang talking about the way she wrote characters from her family into her debut novel *Bestiary*, and I'm sure I'm misremembering it, but she said something about writing fan fiction for one's own life. I think that's what this poem is. It's a combination of a memory I have of my friend falling off her bike and this wish I have that I would have known, sooner and more confidently, that I am queer. On the one hand, it probably would have been painfully lonely to know such a thing in the town that I grew up in—on the other, I often feel like I ignored so many manifestations of my queerness and that I missed out on something. This poem also addresses a fear that because I now openly identify as queer that maybe something innocent, like kissing a friend, was not as innocent as I previously thought, that I was some kind of monster—did I make her kiss me? I think this fear is based on internalized homophobia, but in another way it's just a continuation of feeling not accepted or acceptable. It's what happens when you realize the reality you experience is different from someone else's, and your certainty is destabilized. Still, I broke the line of the title and ended the poem on the hill to indicate some semblance of hope, some resolve to be open to all parts of oneself."

SETH MACGREGOR is a writer and musician from the unceded territory of the Syilx people in the Okanagan, now living in Tiohti:áke/Montreal. His work has appeared in *Grain*, *Headlight*, and is forthcoming in *CV2*.

Of "House Fire on Cook Road," MacGregor writes, "After I graduated from my Christian high school, I worked for a construction restoration company, Stutters, which dealt with insurance claims for properties affected by floods, fires, asbestos, corpses, etc. I felt out of place working there, an effeminate, repressed queer man. I wrote this poem after a conversation about the Gothic, the uncanny, thresholds. I thought of this house I had worked at, which was devastated by a fire. There was so much evidence of the lives that had lived there, and I remember feeling like I was piecing together the house with each bag of garbage I threw away, storying the artifacts that were left behind. And then, peeling open what felt like a threshold, a repression of the house. The poem came from that, an encounter with something without context, trying to understand it, frame it. And it became, I think, a sort of mirror for myself at that time."

SADIE MCCARNEY is the Charlottetown-based author of *Live Ones* (University of Regina Press, 2019/ tall-lighthouse UK, 2020) and *Your Therapist Says It's Magical Thinking* (ECW Press, 2023), as well as the found poetry performance text/mental health memoir *Head War* (Frog Hollow Press, 2021). Her work has appeared in publications including *The Walrus*, *Canadian Literature*, *Foglifter*, and *Grain* (where this poem originally appeared).

Of "Self-Portrait as Diana, Virgin Goddess of the Moon and the Hunt," McCarney writes, "I engage with the world as a queer and asexual woman because I want desperately to connect with others. But when I date, for example, I also find myself at least once or twice removed from the person sitting directly in front of me. This poem is a loose mind map of that experience, of searching anywhere and everywhere in my life for 'the idea of a girlfriend' but overlooking the very real possibilities right in front of me. I ended up tapping in the Roman/Neo-Pagan goddess Diana as an anti-sex symbol, maybe naively hoping that some of her righteous virtue would rub off onto me."

ERIN MCGREGOR is a Settler/Metis writer from Alberta, newly relocated to Winnipeg. Her work has appeared in numerous magazines and her first poetry collection, *What Fills Your House Like Smoke* is forthcoming from Thistledown Press. McGregor currently works as the Director of Culture & Heritage for the Manitoba Metis Federation.

McGregor writes, "'a eulogy' is about the death of a mentor and friend who defied a terminal diagnosis for two years to squeeze out every last drop of this life. Our relationship had always been based on words: meandering conversations, collaborative writing, and comparing notes on books. He was my first and best editor, teaching me to use three words instead of seven (a lesson I continue to struggle with) and to always seek the heart of the message. During his final days, however, words failed us. I was humbled to witness him still attempting to connect even while seized by waves of pain and exhaustion. Death renders us, reminds us we are vessels for love and suffering, nothing more. I wanted to capture some of that feeling and the way our compulsion to contain death in language is swept aside by the physicality of it, and the urgency to communicate love by other, more direct means."

ANNA MOORE is a writer who grew up in Sooke, British Columbia. She studied writing at the University of Victoria and is currently working on a project about the emotional landscapes of galleries and museums.

Of "PKOLS Equinox," Moore writes, "This poem was written close to the moment in which it happened—I was sitting on the beach with a notebook, waiting for my friends, and saw two children interacting with the shoreline environment in a way that brought up some strong childhood memories for me. This was at the tail-end of one of the recent extreme wildfire seasons we've been experiencing in BC. The stifling sensation of the smog on that day brought the intensity of childhood dreams into greater relief, as I held my younger self in one hand and the unexpected realities of growing up into the climate crisis in the other."

RHIANNON NG CHENG HIN is a writer from Quebec. Her debut poetry collection *Fire Cider Rain* was released by Coach House Books in 2022, and her essays and poems have appeared in *Brick Literary Journal, Grain, The Malahat Review, Plenitude*

Magazine, *Arc Poetry Magazine*, and elsewhere. She studies medicine at McGill University.

Of "Telephone Repairman," Ng Cheng Hin writes, "I wrote this poem in memory of my grandad, who worked as a telephone pole repairman in rural northern Scotland for much of his life. He had a story about a hammer he once forgot at one of his work sites, up a little mountain north of Inverness. Nearly twenty years later, my sister and I happened to be walking with him in the area, and he went back to retrieve it. It was still there—rusted, splintered, and buried in dirt and grass, but still there. This poem is a reflection on the stillness and the gentle permanence of both the highland landscape and my grandad's memory. Telephone poles are such silent, mundane, lonely things, yet they channel sound and conversation—they are part of the roar of the everyday. The quiet certainty with which my grandad led his life, 'drifting from pole to pole' between patches of heather and roadside moors, felt dissonant to the noise and bustle that his job facilitated. I wanted to write about that dissonance, and the desperate longing for quiet and stillness that I think many of us feel at times."

BARBARA NICKEL grew up in Saskatchewan and now lives and writes in Yarrow, British Columbia, on the Stó:lo territory of the Pilalt and Ts'elxwéyeqw. Her latest novel is *Dear Peter, Dear Ulla* (Thistledown Press, 2021), winner of the High Plains Book Award and shortlisted for many awards including a BC and Yukon Book Prize. Her latest poetry collection is *Essential Tremor* (Caitlin Press, 2021); her work has appeared in many publications including *Best Canadian Poetry 2021* and *The Walrus*.

Of "Three-in-One," Nickel writes, "A bird surprised me and my family inside the Neolithic tomb of Maeshowe on the Orkney

Islands; she had flown along the entrance tunnel, interrupting our guide's words to feed her babies on a high shelf of the central chamber. The image of open beaks and beating hearts, a resident nest in the centre of a burial mound, became the core of a sonnet that became the centre of a three-part poem that turns on this life-in-death paradox. Turns because in the spirit of John Donne's 'La Corona' (a crown of sonnets), the last words of part one are the first words of part two, the last phrase of two is the first phrase of three, the last phrase of three is the first line of one, and so on round and round, like the cycle of seasons in Eve's winter garden, the seed of which came to me one crisp December morning in the garden, in a kind of paradise as I pulled weeds, thinking of the essential beauty and pain of imperfection and the way compost feeds the soil. I linked this to the death of a young boy on the trail near my home, and a potter friend who had been asked to make his urn. Another potter, also a friend, creates pieces from local Chilliwack River clay. An image of this clay turning in her hands reminded me of origins and the way we are tended and tend, which brings me back to the bird again."

PETER NORMAN lives in Toronto. He is the author of a novel, a forthcoming children's book, and four poetry collections, most recently *Some of Us and Most of You Are Dead* (Wolsak and Wynn, 2018). His first book was a finalist for the 2010 Trillium Book Award for Poetry, and he has appeared in two previous editions of *Best Canadian Poetry*.

Norman writes, "'The Hollowing' was written in response to a call for submissions: a literary journal announced an upcoming theme issue titled 'Sprawl.' I'd been casting about for poetry prompts, and this seemed like a good one; I figured I'd write something about suburbs. But a poem, I find, can be like a strong, stubborn dog. You think you're walking the dog, but suddenly it tugs you down an unfamiliar alley, maybe because it smells a treat or spots a fleeing rodent. Instead of a poem about suburban sprawl, I ended up with a claustrophobic piece of fiction. The phenomenon of hoarding had been prominent in my thoughts, in part because of a recent conversation with someone who'd had to clean out a home where an elderly couple had lived and hoarded. As the poem progressed, I found myself trying to build phrases that might embody the sense of density and excess and decay—and, ultimately, sadness—this guy's story had conveyed. A counterweight to the bleakness was my inherent fascination with jumbled assortments of random stuff. I guess I did manage to slip the word 'sprawl' into the last line, but the finished poem was barely on theme. And, indeed, it was rejected by the journal whose announcement had inspired it, only to find a very happy home in *The New Quarterly*."

TOLU OLORUNTOBA lives in Surrey, British Columbia. He is the author of *Each One a Furnace* (McClelland & Stewart, 2022) (a Dorothy Livesay Poetry Prize finalist) and *The Junta of Happenstance* (Palimpsest, 2021) (winner of the Governor General's Prize for English Language Poetry and the Canadian Griffin Poetry Prize).

Of "Heel Poem / Black-Hooded," Oloruntoba writes, "The 'Heel' in 'Heel Poem' is from wrestling, as delivered to me by the 80s and 90s–era World Wrestling Federation. Having struggled with poor mental health since I was a teenager, I have often defiantly wished that one of the poems I write become villainous, abandon half measures, and take a folding chair to my depression's turned back. In this way, the poem owes a problematic debt to Amiri Baraka's potent, violent, and often unpleasant poem, 'Black Art' ('we want ... "poems that kill" ... Poems that shoot / Guns'). A debt is a debt, although I am made extremely uncomfortable by this juxtaposition because of the poem's (and the poet's) racism, misogyny, and homophobia, which I name and denounce. Jericho Brown also personifies the poem in 'Duplex,' as an entity making 'dark demands.' Personifying one of my diagnoses in this way helps me externalize (and hopefully thereby contain) it by asking my poetry to become incarnate. I had been writing a long sequence of finch poems, and the 'Black-Hooded' in the title refers to the 'Black-Hooded Sierra Finch.' A dastardly and unsavoury character like I was invoking might wear a black hood, and sneak into the arena to do its necessary evil. Perhaps some good, however little, can be salvaged from the bad."

MICHAEL ONDAATJE was born in Sri Lanka and lives in Toronto. He is the author of several award-winning novels, as well as a memoir, a nonfiction book on film, and several books of poetry. Among other accolades, his novel *The English Patient* won the Booker Prize, and *Anil's Ghost* won the *Irish Times* International Fiction Prize, the Giller prize, and the Prix Médicis.

JANA PRIKRYL was born in the former Czechoslovakia and immigrated to Canada as a child. She is the author of *Midwood* (2022), *No Matter* (2019), and *The After Party* (2016), and has received fellowships from the Guggenheim Foundation and the Radcliffe Institute as well as an Award in Literature from the

American Academy of Arts and Letters. Prikryl is the executive editor of the *New York Review of Books*.

MATT RADER lives in Kelowna, British Columbia. He's the author of five collections of poems, most recently, *Ghosthawk* (Nightwood, 2021). He teaches Creative Writing at the University of British Columbia, Okanagan.

Rader writes, "On June 29, 2021, the temperature reached a record-breaking 46.7 degrees in Kelowna. The cultural milieu at the time was also very heated. The pandemic continued unabated. Vaccines had only been widely available for a few months and the backlash was growing. The discovery of 215 unmarked graves at the former Kamloops Residential School, only 100 kilometres from Kelowna, had been announced a few weeks prior. Several churches in the region had been deliberately set ablaze. 'Heat Dome' is a fairly literal account of what I did, thought, and felt that morning."

MONTY REID was born in Saskatchewan and now lives in Ottawa. His collections include *The Luskville Reductions* (Brick Books), *Garden* (Chaudiere Books) and *Crawlspace* (House of Anansi) as well as the chapbooks from several small presses. He has won a variety of awards and been shortlisted for the GG on three occasions. For many years he was the managing editor of *Arc Poetry Magazine* and was also the long-time director of VerseFest, Ottawa's international poetry festival.

Reid writes, "'Spring Rider' is a small poem from a larger collection called *Playground*, which is an engagement with the many and various structures we create for our kids, and our adults, to play in. My interest was piqued when the playground at my daughter's school was vandalized and burned to the ground. I played a small role in the committee charged with raising funds for a rebuild. It took a while, but we were successful, and the playground, much enhanced, has since reopened. But the complexity, and the cost, of playground materials and structures was a surprise to all of us and it made me start wondering about many of the other places—bouncy castles, escape rooms, ziplines, poetry magazines, etc.—where we play."

LISA RICHTER is a poet, writer, and educator living in Tkaronto/Toronto. She is the author of the poetry collections *Closer to Where We Began* (Tightrope Books, 2017) and *Nautilus and Bone* (Frontenac House, 2020), winner of the National Jewish Book Award for Poetry (US) and the Canadian Jewish Literary Award for Poetry, amongst other honours. She is currently pursuing an MFA in Creative Writing at the University of Guelph.

Richter writes, "'Whatever It Takes' takes its title from a line from the movie *Win-Win*, in which the runaway teen who has become the unlikely star of his high school wrestling team describes his process by saying, 'I have to do whatever the fuck it takes to get out [alive].' This line became a personal mantra of mine, a rallying call for strength, courage, and perseverance during difficult times. It came back to me when I was searching for a title for this poem, which I wrote in the second year of the pandemic. The poem, I think, proposes a certain negative capability, which Keats defined as having the ability to 'accept uncertainties, mysteries, doubts, without any irritable reaching after fact and reason.' I think of negative capability as the antidote to both toxic positivity and defeatism, which are two sides of the same coin. We can both grieve a lost parent and acknowledge their quirks, flaws and idiosyncrasies. We can sit in fear and discomfort in a hospital waiting room and admire a stranger's choice of footwear. Anxiety, fear, and restlessness can and do coexist with joy, tenderness, and wonder."

MEAGHAN RONDEAU exists in Vancouver. She works an increasingly demoralizing regular job that she hopes to have convinced herself to quit by the time this anthology is published. Her poems, nonfiction, and unfaithful translations from dead languages have appeared in and/or been rejected by enough lit mags that you have to think she'll get it together and put a book out at some point. I mean, she's 43, for crying out loud.

Rondeau writes, "Hello and welcome to my paragraph! 'Portrait of the Author Fucking' etc. is part of a set. It got accepted on the first try but the other two get rejected wherever they go. I think one of the rejects is actually better than this one, objectively, but there's no logic to what gets published and what doesn't. Anyway, this poem was inspired by an EOA (evening of awkwardness) that happened in early 2013. I was at least 50 percent responsible for the said awkwardness, as the poem hopefully makes clear. One reason I write is that I'm often detached from my feelings in the moment, especially if the moment sucks, so if I want that information, I have to extract it after the fact. Another reason is that by translating an experience into words I can give myself (and others) the impression that I was in control of the situation at the time, when I (and probably others) know damn well that really what I'm in control of is language afterward, which is cool in its own way but not at all the same thing, and this distinction and my awareness of it generate a lot of the tension/splitness driving this poem. In it, I manipulate and annoy the reader, you, in many of my favourite ways: disrespecting the space-time continuum, swearing, committing fourth-wall atrocities, having people reveal themselves in their own words, and most importantly sneaking at least one cat onto the page for no actual reason."

OLAJIDE SALAWU lives in Edmonton. He is the author of *Preface for Leaving Homeland* published under African Poetry Book Fund. He is also a PhD student in English and Film Studies. His individual poems have appeared in journals across Canadian venues such as *Grain*, *Contemporary Verse 2*, *Literary Review of Canada*, *The Ex-Puritan*, and so on.

Olajide writes, "The original inspiration of my poem's title came from Kei Miller's 'The Cartographer Maps a Way to Zion.' Although I do not think my poem and Miller's work address the same context. When I wrote 'A Cartographer Maps His Way Out of His Country,' I was thinking about the recent exodus and drain of Nigerian youth population. The cartographer is the Nigerian youth who has been displaced and sent on exile because of social economic condition and brutal hardship of living where the social class chasm continues to widen. Yet, a cartographer can also be more. They are the labour migrants of the professional class who are lured into the Western programs of migration and economic soft-landing. I was thinking about all of these, while also pondering about myself as a cartographer, a Black migrant student. I have intentionally brought Nigerian idioms and Pidgin such as 'trenches' into use to foreground the peculiarity of its Nigerian-ness, and if you wish the Africanness of this problem. Also, one can trace the thematic pedigree of the poem in the last line to Ben Okri's *The Famished Road*, which also grounds its Nigerian context. I think this poem underwent three drafts. The first draft was written during my fellowship with Vancouver Manuscript Intensive Fellowship. The other versions were written in the dark room of my house on 81 Avenue, Edmonton."

FRANCESCA SCHULZ-BIANCO is a Canadian writer currently living in Berlin. A finalist in *The Sewanee Review* Poetry Contest in 2021, she also has recent poems in *The Malahat Review*.

Schulz-Bianco writes: "I wrote this poem during the pandemic, at a time when I lived on the internet. I was preoccupied with the strangeness of being in a physical body and the way we speak about it metaphorically. I also watched, with great anxiety, as social media started to promote the revision of our physical features. And so I sat down to write something that could remind me of my body's inherent value and potential. The poem was first inspired by poets I love who write about the body, and partly uses found language gathered by typing keywords ('My body is ...') into a search engine. For instance, the title comes from a blog post on weight loss, and the 'ultimate gift for future generations' line is drawn from an organ donation website. These uncanny fragments were then put into conversation with my inner world, both its existential musings and memories. There are sacred spots I would often dream about while in lockdown, not knowing whether I'd ever revisit them in person again. The Valley of the Temples in Agrigento, Sicily, is one of those places. Near that ancient site is the promise of the ocean below, where one can imagine maritime archaeologists hauling oxidized bronze statues out onto the sand. '10 easy steps to my body' takes a bird's-eye look at the speaker's various states— from the moment of birth to death—and asks: how many selves will we discover, inhabit, and abandon in this lifetime?"

JAMES SCOLES lives in Winnipeg. He is the author of *The Trailer* (Signature Editions, 2021). He has lived, travelled, and worked in over ninety countries, and a short memoir of his time in Japan is forthcoming (Fish Publishing, 2023) in Ireland. His poem "The Trailer" won the 2013 CBC Poetry Prize and his short stories are featured in *Coming Attractions 13* (Oberon Press, 2013). Scoles teaches creative writing & literature at the University of Winnipeg. Learn more: jamesscoles.ca

Scoles writes, "'Last Train Home' was originally part of my travel poetry collection (currently seeking a home)—*The Stone Roses of Sarajevo*—that takes the reader around the world, much as *The Trailer* (Signature Editions, 2021) brought the reader into the trailer park world. When writing my travel poetry, I revisited my journals and notes from my years in Japan, and this poem was crafted from a scribbled first draft on the last train home one night in Tokyo: 'I'm a buzzing, dying florescent tube as two lovers duck out of our train just as the doors close and make for a nearby love hotel. Tonight I'll dream of cut-up cartoon cows and monkeys and tomorrow teach pharmaceutical executives how to present their unpleasant research in the most pleasing way.' I was instantly transported back to Japan, in time and place, to a giant pharmaceutical complex and testing lab, where my coworkers took me on a tour of the facility that ended with me passing out shortly after entering and seeing hundreds of caged animals hooked up to hoses and machines. I wanted the poem to reveal the industry and the speaker's trauma and recurring nightmares (I used to have the odd nightmare from that experience, nearly twenty years ago, but haven't since I wrote the poem). Those scribbled first lines accessed the deep memory that led to the poetic capture of the experience in 'Last Train

Home,' now the title poem of a whole new collection of poems, all set in Japan."

ALLAN SERAFINO is a writer from Calgary, Alberta. His poems have appeared in over fifty Canadian, American, UK, and Australian magazines and in three collections: *Troubled Dreams*, *Alien States*, and *Another Way* (Exstasis Editions). He has also published two young adult novels (LTD Books). He was the former editor and president of *Dandelion/blue buffalo* magazines and founding president of The Calgary Writers Association.

Allan writes, "The poem 'Hare' began with the Buddhist jataka—literally, 'birth story'—that refers to the many reincarnations of Buddha mostly in the form of animals. Though not a Buddhist myself, I can ask, 'Is the lowly hare in my backyard a form of Buddha? What is he saying to me?' Squirrels, sparrows, and other animals now leave clues for me about myself like the fact that I know nothing. That is clear. Buddhist poems have tended to be short, aphoristic, with simple lines and observations. They dare us to wonder and to doubt and then laugh about it. Doubt is the clearest form of knowing that we know."

SUE SINCLAIR grew up in Newfoundland on Beothuk territory, and she is the author of six collections of poetry, including her latest book, *Almost Beauty: New and Selected Poems* (Goose Lane Editions, 2022). All of Sue's books have won or been nominated for a variety of awards. Sue has a PhD in philosophy and teaches creative writing at the University of New Brunswick on Wolastoqiyik territory.

Of "The Nashwaak River," Sinclair writes, "The Nashwaak River flows into the Wolastoq, in whose valley I now live. One day when we were out walking, my daughter asked, 'Is the river safe to swim in?' I didn't know but did some research and discovered that the answer is 'for now.' The huge mine referred to in the note to the poem had just days ago been approved by the federal government. The environmental impact report, quoted in the poem, left much to be desired. I turned to poetry to process what I'd learned and was experiencing. I studied beauty for years as a philosophy student, and I remain deeply attuned to experiences of beauty; among other things, I was aware that looming mine had warped my experience of the river's beauty. There is, however, a happy postscript: thanks to community efforts, thousands of native trees (willows and silver maples) are being planted along the banks to better anchor them against flooding. Shout out to the Nashwaak Watershed Association!"

CAROLYN SMART lives on a wooded property north of Kingston, Ontario, and is the author of six volumes of poetry and a memoir. Her most recent collections are *Hooked* and *Careen*, both from Brick Books. For thirty-two years she taught Creative Writing at Queen's University, is the founder of the RBC Bronwen Wallace Award, and is dedicated to helping emerging writers through her editorial and mentoring services. www.carolynsmartediting.ca

Smart writes, "'Ashes' speaks to one aspect of the complex and surprising experience of grief. It is dedicated to my two sons and my stepson. The envy of his friends for his many capabilities and robust health, my husband was diagnosed without apparent symptoms for a disease that took his life within a year. I cared for him at home until his death, and days later received his ashes in a plastic bag within a paper shopping bag. The surreal situation and my intense grief make up the core of this poem. I now live in a landscape filled with his presence, and often feel as if he has become what surrounds me since his ashes lie in the field nearby under trees. Two years after his death, the land is bursting into blossom once again.

MISHA SOLOMON is a poet in and of Tiohtià:ke/Montréal. He is the author of two chapbooks, *FLORALS* (above/ground press, 2020) and *Full Sentences* (Turret House Press, 2022), and his work has also appeared in journals including *The /tƐmz/ Review*, *Yolk*, *Vallum*, and *Plenitude Magazine*. He is currently pursuing his MA at Concordia University.

Of "I'm a hole / I'm a pole / My great-grandmother was a Pole," Solomon writes, "This poem began as a response to a prompt from experimental poet Sarah Burgoyne to 'write a poem of unbelievable symbolic effort.' As a homosexual Jew, I'm interested in exploring facets of my identity in uncomfortably literal ways. What would happen if I broke my body down into the simplest shapes and symbols? What would happen if I did the same thing to familial history, much of which was lost in flight? I treasure holes and poles equally—and if my therapist is reading this, I treasure our time together."

JOHN STEFFLER was born in Toronto and, after many years in Newfoundland, now lives in eastern Ontario on unceded traditional Omàmìwininì (Algonquin) territory. His books include two novels, a children's book, a collection of essays (*Forty-One Pages: on Poetry, Language and Wilderness*, URP 2019) and seven collections of poems, the most recent being *And Yet* (M&S, 2020). From 2006 to 2009 he was Poet Laureate of Canada.

Steffler writes, "The subject of this poem is part of my broad interest in what I think of as the wilderness within us—the things we don't fully understand or fully control in ourselves, in our minds and actions, in our desires, weaknesses, impulses, aversions, intuitions, and blind spots. 'Unwelcome Scene' is about the clichéd concept of *one's worst fear*. What do our worst fears tell us about ourselves? Why have them at all? Do we unconsciously attract their fulfillment? Are they proxies—something like psychic symbols—for our inevitable losses and letting go? I've had the experience of seeing some of my worst fears realized. I've survived this, so far. In form and organization, I wanted this poem to be not loose and impressionistic but tight and relentless, driven, to give the feeling of being compelled to face a bitter truth, a challenge, which for me is one of the main impulses for writing poetry and in general for making art—how to deal with our worst fears whether experienced in imagination or for real."

JOHN ELIZABETH STINTZI (they/she) is a trans poet, novelist, cartoonist, and photographer who grew up on a cattle farm in northwestern Ontario. They are the author of the poetry collection *Junebat* (House of Anansi, 2020), the novels *My Volcano* (Arsenal Pulp Press, 2022) and *Vanishing Monuments* (Arsenal Pulp Press, 2020), and the comic *Automaton Deactivation Bureau*. They are the winner of the 2019 Bronwen Wallace Award for poetry and the inaugural Sator New Works Award from Two Dollar Radio.

Stintzi writes, "I can't recall the exact moment I wrote 'I Left the Boy Forever,' but it's a companion to another poem titled 'I Left the Farm Forever,' from which 'Boy' borrows the same first clause ('I left the farm forever / once'), but instead with the word boy replacing farm. I wanted to write about the feeling of leaving something you can never really leave, that you can never really excise yourself (by which I mean myself) from completely. The poem is part of a collection I'm writing called *The Farm Boy Parallels*, which is about what it means (to me) to leave home. It's about how these various home-spaces—of which I would include gender—can feel either inhospitable or simply not sufficient, despite that there are many things you love deeply about them. With this poem specifically, I address the gender-as-home alongside the farm. To me, the problem with being a man was that I felt wholly incompatible with masculinity—which life on the farm made all the clearer. What I needed from gender was more: more space, more dimensions, more contradiction. But, of course, my personal experience of trying to leave 'boy' behind is a process that haunts me, and one which I must repeat. It is rare that I'm seen as myself, and thus am 'ever dragged back / in the gaze of the world' and must, every morning, 'rise / to the warm light / of *his* burning.'"

JOANNA STREETLY has lived in the traditional territory of the Tla-o-qui-aht on the west coast of Vancouver Island since 1990. She is the published author of four books and has been listed for the FBCW Literary Writes Poetry Contest, the Canada Writes Creative Non-fiction Prize, and *The Spectator*'s Shiva Naipaul award. Her work appears in literary magazines, anthologies, and *Best Canadian Essays 2017*. From 2018–2020 she was the inaugural Tofino Poet Laureate.

Streetly writes, "One June morning in 2018, I and many others began searching—by motorboat, kayak, even on foot—for three young Tla-o-qui-aht men whose boat had vanished two hundred metres from the dock. Two of those men were my stepsons. I'd lived with them for seven years, from when they were small enough to sit on my lap until they were old enough to squirm away. Now in their thirties, I'd last seen them only a few days before. That morning, full moon and spring tides created the lowest water of the year. Caught in the current's extreme grip, the boys had likely been swept miles out to sea. But maybe not? Javelins of light pierced the crown of the rainforest, struck the water, bounced off the gleaming seaweed. Everything was alive with newness. Even my task was new. I was looking for—what was I looking for? A hand waving, a person stranded on the rocks, a body submerged? As I paddled my kayak, a wolf paused at the edge of an island, staring out to sea, paws in the water. Was it showing me where to look? Or was it simply observing the beauty of the sunrise, paying homage to the longest days of the year? Everywhere I looked there were signs like this. In lieu of finding the boys, I collected the signs. And over the months and years of fruitless searching, these signs began to populate my writing, eventually settling into this poem, 'Gyre.'"

ROB TAYLOR lives in Port Moody, British Columbia, on the unceded territory of the Kwikwetlem and Tsleil-Waututh peoples. His fifth poetry collection, *Weather*, will be published by Gaspereau Press in Spring 2024.

Taylor writes, "Our daughter was less than a year old when the COVID-19 lockdown began. The already small orbit of our life cinched tighter, and my poems shrank with it. I thought of poems as I pushed the stroller or spooned baby food, repeating them in my mind until I was able to put pen to paper (most often after the children were asleep). The few poems that survived to the end of the day emerged polished from my mental rock tumbler. The day I wrote 'Sunlight' was a lucky one. I composed it on my hike back up the mountain, and revised it on the way down. When I reached the parking lot, my family was waiting, safe and warm and patient with me as I fumbled for my notebook."

SARAH YI-MEI TSIANG lives in Kingston, Ontario, and is the author of *Grappling Hook* (Palimpsest, 2022), which was short-listed for the Raymond Souster Award, *Status Update* (Oolichan Books, 2013), shortlisted for the Pat Lowther Award, and the Gerald Lampert Award–winning *Sweet Devilry* (Oolichan Books, 2011). She is the poetry editor for *Arc Poetry Magazine*, the creative director of Poetry In Voice, and teaches creative writing at Queens University and through the Vancouver Manuscript Intensive.

Tsiang writes, "I wrote 'The air, then' when I was pregnant in 2020. I hadn't expected the virus or the baby and everything seemed so precarious and uncertain. Who was I to be bringing a child into such a world? This poem came about in a series of confessional poems I wrote when I discovered I was pregnant. Pregnancy is such a liminal time and it is fraught with fears of death, miscarriage, and general anxiety about the future. Yet it is also a deeply hopeful time filled with the promise of life and joy. In many ways my feelings about COVID and quarantine would swing between these two states: terror and hope."

JAMES WARNER lives in Halifax. His poems have been appearing for many years in literary magazines throughout Canada, and occasionally abroad.

Warner writes, "'Dame Philosophy' was first composed so long ago that I can't remember its circumstances, nor the extent to which the dream described has been altered in the writing. I seem to remember there was a dream. And there was indeed a reading, or attempted reading, of Boethius' famous book. My title refers to that disembodied figure Boethius addresses in some of his pages—that *she* who may be thought of as the spirit of philosophy, or a princesse lointaine *avant la lettre*, or perhaps, as some speculate, his beloved wife, whom he was never to see again. Of one thing, we can be sure: the airport mentioned towards the end of my poem is definitely LAX."

ELANA WOLFF lives and works in Thornhill, Ontario—the traditional lands of the Haudenosaunee and Huron-Wendat First Nations. Elana's writing has recently appeared in *Arc Poetry Magazine*, CV2, *FreeFall*, *Galaxy Brain*, *Literary Review of Canada*, *Montréal Serai*, *The New Quarterly*, *Pinhole Poetry*, *Prairie Fire*, *Taddle Creek*, *Vallum*, and *Yolk*. Her collection, *Swoon*, received the 2020 Canadian Jewish Literary Award for Poetry. Her cross-genre Kafka-quest work, *Faithfully Seeking Franz*, is forthcoming from Guernica Editions.

Wolff writes, "'Concern for Soul Consumes Me' is a meditative homage that takes its title from a true concern of mine: the workings of the spirit/ual or immaterial, animating force in human beings and animals, that may be regarded as indestructible. The italicized words are drawn from the posthumous collection, *Notes Without a Text*, by Roberto Bazlen (1902–1965); translated by Alex Andriesse and edited and introduced by Roberto Calasso (Dublin: Dalkey Archive Press, 2019:164; 204). Bazlen published none of his own writing during his lifetime but was an adviser to Italian publishing houses, a translator of Freud and Jung, and a deep reader of Franz Kafka; as was Calasso, as am I. Kafka—now long in the hereafter—struggled with breathing for the last seven years of his fraught life, and died young (in 1924) of laryngeal tuberculosis when he could no longer eat, drink, or speak. The lines, 'Kafka— / whose rendering of difficult things / was easier for him, it seems to me, / than birthing breath' represent an unverifiable surmise. And yet the closing lines of the poem—in invoking the catalpa trees, the spotted woodpecker and his crimson cap—make an ardent and unapologetic claim for poetic conjecture, (implicit) faith, and teachers / mentors (even inanimate) of any persuasion.

NOTABLE POEMS

Susan Glickman, "Green Tomatoes," *The Antigonish Review* 209

Jesse Holth, "Bodies," PRISM *international* 60.2

Danielle Hubbard, "The muse hunt," *Geist* 121

Alex Jennings, "Notes from Old Carthage," EVENT 50.3

Erin Knight, "Paper Plane," *Literary Review of Canada* October 2022

Zoë Landale, "Search and rescue callout before breakfast: 'We have a 16 to 18 ft vessel not under command, drifting up Plumper Sound'," EVENT 51.1

Grace Lau, "That Time I Called An Auntie A Bitch," *The New Quarterly* 161

karen lee, "Ginnal," *Room* 45.2

Louie Leyson, "killing flies in late september," *The Malahat Review* 219

Victoria Mbabazi, "A Study in Mourning," *Room* 45.1

Shane Neilson, "Definitional," *The Antigonish Review* 208

Catherine Owen, "Necessity: a caudate glosa on Frank Bidart," *The Antigonish Review* 211

Kelly Rose Pflug-Black, "Surfacing," *Augur Magazine* 5.1

James Pollock, "Framing Hammer," *The Fiddlehead* 291

Michael Prior, "Saba," *Brick* 109

Tara McGowan-Ross, "gajjamu'g wasueg," *The Fiddlehead* 290

Luke Sawczak, "Little Candles," *The Nashwaak Review* 46/47

Jennifer Shelby, "Mother/Murder," *Augur* 5.1

Mazzy Sleep, "Heart Medicine," *Geist* 122

Anne Swannell, "Prediction," *Literary Review of Canada* October 2022

Elina Taillon, "Late Stages," *Augur* 5.2

Sara Truuvert, "Real Magic," *Room* 45.1

Andrew Wei, "Shrine," EVENT 50.3

Catriona Wright, "Luna Moth," *Arc Poetry Magazine* 98

Laura Zacharin, "Sonnet for Everything," *The Windsor Review* 54.2

Bänoo Zan, "Creation Story," *Prairie Fire* 43.1

Hava Zitlalik, "Inheritance," PRISM *international* 61.1

MAGAZINES CONSULTED

Each year, the fifty best poems and the list of notable poems by Canadian poets are selected from more than sixty print and online journals published in the previous year. While direct submissions of individual poems are not accepted, we welcome review copies from print outlets and announcements of new issues from online publications. Please direct two copies of each print issue to Best Canadian Poetry c/o Biblioasis, 1686 Ottawa St., Ste 100, Windsor, ON N8Y 1R1, or email us at bestcanadianpoetry@biblioasis.com.

The Antigonish Review (antigonishreview.com). PO Box 5000, Antigonish, NS, B2G 2W5

Arc Poetry Magazine (arcpoetry.ca). PO Box 81060, Ottawa, ON, K1P 1B1

Augur Magazine (augurmag.com)

Brick, A Literary Journal (brickmag.com). PO Box 609, Stn. P, Toronto, ON, M5S 2Y4

Bywords (bywords.ca)

Canadian Broadcasting Corporation, CBC Poetry Prize finalists (cbc.ca)

Canadian Literature. University of British Columbia, 8-6303 N.W. Marine Dr., Vancouver, BC, V6T 1Z1

Canadian Notes & Queries (notesandqueries.ca).1686 Ottawa St., Suite 100, Windsor, ON, N8Y 1R1

Carousel (carouselmagazine.ca). UC 274, University of Guelph, Guelph, ON, N1G 2W1

Carte Blanche (carteblanchemagazine.com)

Contemporary Verse 2 (*CV2*) (contemporaryverse2.ca). 502–100 Arthur St., Winnipeg, MB, R3B 1H3

EVENT (eventmagazine.ca). PO Box 2503, New Westminster, BC, V3L 5B2

The Ex-Puritan (ex-puritan.ca)

Exile Quarterly (theexilewriters.com). Exile/Excelsior Publishing Inc., 170 Wellington St. W., PO Box 308, Mount Forest, ON, N0G 2L0

Existere (yorku.ca/existere). Vanier College 101E, York University, 4700 Keele St. Toronto, ON, M3J 1P3

Feathertale (feathertale.com/review). PO Box 5023, Ottawa, ON, K2C 3H3

The Fiddlehead (thefiddlehead.ca). Campus House, University of New Brunswick, 11 Garland Ct., PO Box 4400, Fredericton, NB, E3B 5A3

filling Station (fillingstation.ca). PO Box 22135, Bankers Hall, Calgary, AB, T2P 4J5

FreeFall (freefallmagazine.ca). 250 Maunsell Close, NE Calgary, AB T2E 7C2

Geist (geist.com). Suite 210, 111 W. Hastings St., Vancouver, BC, V6B 1H4

Grain (grainmagazine.ca). PO Box 3986, Regina, SK, S4P 3R9

HA&L (*Hamilton Arts & Letters Magazine*) (halmagazine. wordpress.com)

Juniper Poetry (juniperpoetry.com)

Literary Review of Canada (reviewcanada.ca). 340 King St. E., Toronto, ON, M5A 1K8

long con magazine (longconmag.com)

Maisonneuve (maisonneuve.org). 1051 boul. Decarie, PO Box 53527, Saint Laurent, QC, H4L 5J9

The Malahat Review (malahatreview.ca). University of Victoria, PO Box 1700, Stn. CSC, Victoria, BC, V8W 2Y2

Minola Review (minolareview.com)

The Nashwaak Review (stu.ca/english/the-nashwaak-review). St. Thomas University, Fredericton, NB, E3B 5G3

The New Quarterly (tnq.ca). St. Jerome's University, 290 Westmount Rd. N., Waterloo, ON, N2L 3G3

Open Minds Quarterly (openmindsquarterly.com)

Parentheses (parenthesesjournal.com)

Periodicities (periodicityjournal.blogspot.com)

Plenitude Magazine (plenitudemagazine.ca)

Poetry Pause (poets.ca/poetrypause)

Poetry Review (poetrysociety.org.uk/publications-section/the-poetry-review). 22 Betterton Street, London, UK, WC2H 9BX

Prairie Fire (prairiefire.ca). 423–100 Arthur St., Winnipeg, MB, R3B 1H3

PRISM international (prismmagazine.ca). Creative Writing Program, University of British Columbia, Buchanan Room E462, 1866 Main Mall, Vancouver, BC, V6T 1Z1

Queen's Quarterly (queensu.ca/quarterly). Queen's University, 144 Barrie St., Kingston, ON, K7L 3N6

Ricepaper (ricepapermagazine.ca). PO Box 74174, Hillcrest RPO, Vancouver, BC, V5V 5L8

Riddle Fence (riddlefence.com)

Room (roommagazine.com). PO Box 46160, Stn. D, Vancouver, BC, V6J 5G5

subTerrain (subterrain.ca). PO Box 3008, MPO, Vancouver, BC, V6B 3X5

Taddle Creek (taddlecreekmag.com). PO Box 611, Stn. P, Toronto, ON, M5S 2Y4

The /tɛmz/ Review (thetemzreview.com)

This Magazine (this.org). 417–401 Richmond St. W., Toronto, ON, M5V 3A8

Train: a poetry journal (trainpoetryjournal.blogspot.com)

Vallum (vallummag.com). 5038 Sherbrooke W., PO Box 23077, CP Vendome, Montreal, QC, H4A 1T0

The Walrus (walrusmagazine.com). 411 Richmond St. E., Suite B15, Toronto, ON, M5A 3S5

West End Phoenix (westendphoenix.com). The Gladstone Hotel, 1214 Queen St. W., Toronto, ON, M6J 1J6

The Windsor Review (ojs.uwindsor.ca). Department of English, University of Windsor, 401 Sunset Ave., Windsor, ON N9B 3P4

INDEX TO POETS

ACKNOWLEDGEMENTS

"The air, then" appeared in *The Malahat Review* copyright © Sarah Yi-Mei Tsiang. Reprinted with permission of the author.

"Ashes" appeared in *Grain* copyright © Carolyn Smart. Reprinted with permission of the author.

"Atmospheric River" appeared in *Grain* copyright © Nicholas Bradley. Reprinted with permission of the author.

"Ballad" first appeared in *The Walrus* copyright © Luke Hathaway. Reprinted from *The Affirmations* by Luke Hathaway (Biblioasis, 2022) with permission of the author and publisher.

"Bob Ross Beats the Devil" appeared in *Grain* copyright © David Barrick. Reprinted with permission of the author.

"A Cartographer Maps His Way Out of His Country" appeared in *Grain* copyright © Olajide Salawu. Reprinted with permission of the author.

"Concern for Soul Consumes Me" appeared in the *Literary Review of Canada* copyright © Elana Wolff. Reprinted with permission of the author.

"Dame Philosophy" appeared in *EVENT* copyright © James Warner. Reprinted with permission of the author.

"The Hollowing" appeared in *The New Quarterly* copyright ©
Peter Norman. Reprinted with permission of the author.

"House Fire on Cook Road" appeared in *Grain* copyright ©
Seth MacGregor. Reprinted with permission of the author.

"I Left the Boy Forever" appeared in *Ex-Puritan* copyright ©
John Elizabeth Stintzi. Reprinted with permission of the author.

"I'm a hole / I'm a pole / My great-grandmother was a Pole"
appeared in *The /tɛmz/ Review* copyright © Misha Solomon.
Reprinted with permission of the author.

"Last Things Lasting" appeared in *Qwerty* copyright © Joel
Robert Ferguson. Reprinted with permission of the author.

"Last Train Home" appeared in *Grain* copyright © James
Scoles. Reprinted with permission of the author.

"Little fires" appeared in *The Nashwaak Review* copyright ©
Louise Carson. Reprinted with permission of the author.

"Moving Day" appeared in *Grain* copyright © Susan Gillis.
Reprinted with permission of the author.

"My Muted Year" appeared in *Grain* copyright © Hilary Clark.
Reprinted with permission of the author.

"The Nashwaak River" first appeared in *Prairie Fire* copyright
© Sue Sinclair. Reprinted from *Almost Beauty: New and
Selected Poems* by Sue Sinclair (Goose Lane, 2022) with
permission of the author and publisher.

"A Newly Discovered Species of Lizard with Distinctive
Triangular Scales" first appeared in *Plenitude Magazine*

"Spring Rider" appeared in *filling Station* copyright © Monty Reid. Reprinted with permission of the author.

"Still, Night Thoughts" appeared in PRISM *international* copyright © Erin Conway-Smith. Reprinted with permission of the author.

"A Study in Coats" appeared in *Canadian Literature* copyright © Nina Berkhout. Reprinted with permission of the author.

"Sunlight" appeared in the *Literary Review of Canada* copyright © Rob Taylor. Reprinted with permission of the author.

"Tai Chi in the Snow" appeared in *The Fiddlehead* copyright © Jean Eng. Reprinted with permission of the author.

"Telephone Repairman" appeared in *The Walrus* copyright © Rhiannon Ng Cheng Hin. Reprinted with permission of the author.

"10 easy steps to my body" appeared in *The Malahat Review* copyright © Francesca Schulz-Bianco. Reprinted with permission of the author.

"There Are No Actual Monsters in This Poem I Hope" first appeared in *The Malahat Review* copyright © T. Liem. Reprinted from *Slows: Twice* by T. Liem (Coach House, 2023) with permission of the author and publisher.

"Thirteen Years" appeared in *The New Quarterly* copyright © Kayla Czaga. Reprinted with permission of the author.

"Three-in-One" appeared in *Grain* copyright © Barbara Nickel. Reprinted with permission of the author.

EDITOR BIOGRAPHIES

BARDIA SINAEE's poetry, essays, and book reviews have appeared in magazines throughout Canada. His first book, *Intruder* (House of Anansi, 2021), received the Trillium Book Award for Poetry and was shortlisted for the Gerald Lampert Memorial Award. He was born in Tehran, Iran, and currently lives in Ottawa.

ANITA LAHEY's latest poetry collection is *While Supplies Last* (Véhicule Press, 2023). She's also co-author, with Pauline Conley, of the 2023 graphic novel-in-verse *Fire Monster* (Palimpsest Press). Her 2020 memoir, *The Last Goldfish: a True Tale of Friendship* (Biblioasis), was an Ottawa Book Award finalist. Anita has worked with *Best Canadian Poetry* since 2014, and has served as series editor since 2018. She lives in Ottawa.

Printed by Imprimerie Gauvin
Gatineau, Québec